SHAPED BY SCRIPTURE

The God We Serve

DANIEL

DOUG WARD

Contents

THE *SHAPED BY SCRIPTURE* SERIES

The first step of an organized study of the Bible is the selection of a biblical book, which is not always an easy task. Often people pick a book they are already familiar with, books they think will be easy to understand, or books that, according to popular opinion, seem to have more relevance to Christians today than other books of the Bible. However, it is important to recognize the truth that God's Word is not limited to just a few books. All the biblical books, both individually and collectively, communicate God's Word to us. As Paul affirms in 2 Timothy 3:16, "All Scripture is God-breathed and is useful for teaching, rebuking, correcting and training in righteousness." We interpret the term "God-breathed" to mean inspired by God. If Christians are going to take 2 Timothy 3:16 seriously, then we should all set the goal of encountering God's Word as communicated through all sixty-six books of the Bible. New Christians or those with little to no prior knowledge of the Bible might find it best to start with a New Testament book like 1 John, James, or the Gospel of John.

By purchasing this volume, you have chosen to study the Old Testament book of Daniel. You have made a great choice because this book presents a fascinating mixture of narratives filled with compelling characters, political intrigue, and dangerous exploits; and apocalyptic visions that reflect the world stage in cosmic proportions. Ultimately, these pieces of Daniel's story come together to address some of humanity's deepest, most enduring concerns, such as the meaning of suffering, the struggle against evil, and our ultimate destiny. The goal of this series is to illustrate an appropriate method for studying the Bible, so instead of a comprehensive study of Daniel, this volume will be limited to a few select chapters that have been chosen as representative of the stories and the biblical genre found in the book of Daniel.

How This Study Works

This Bible study is intended for a period of seven weeks. We have chosen a specific passage for each week's study. This study can be done individually or with a small group.

For individual study, we recommend a five-day study each week, following the guidelines given below:

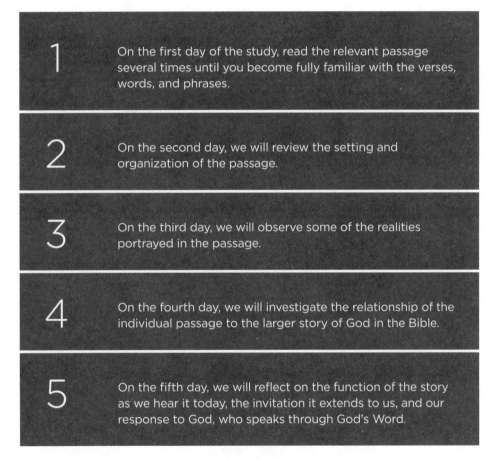

1   On the first day of the study, read the relevant passage several times until you become fully familiar with the verses, words, and phrases.

2   On the second day, we will review the setting and organization of the passage.

3   On the third day, we will observe some of the realities portrayed in the passage.

4   On the fourth day, we will investigate the relationship of the individual passage to the larger story of God in the Bible.

5   On the fifth day, we will reflect on the function of the story as we hear it today, the invitation it extends to us, and our response to God, who speaks through God's Word.

If this Bible study is done as a group activity, we recommend that members of the group meet together on the sixth day to share and discuss what they have learned from God's Word and how it has transformed their lives.

You may want to have a study Bible to give you additional insights as we work through the book of Daniel. Other helpful resources are *Discovering the Old Testament* and *Daniel: A Commentary in the Wesleyan Tradition,* available from The Foundry Publishing.

Literary Forms in the Bible

There are several literary forms represented throughout the Bible. The divinely inspired writers used various techniques to communicate God's Word to their ancient audiences. The major literary forms (also known as genres) of the Bible are:

- narratives

- laws

- history

- Wisdom literature (in the form of dialogues and proverbial statements)

- poetry (consisting of poems of praise, lament, trust in God, and more)

- prophecy

- discourses

- parables

- miracle stories

- letters (also known as epistles)

- exhortations

- apocalyptic writings

Within each of these forms, one may find subgenres. Each volume in the *Shaped by Scripture* series will briefly overview the genres found in the book of the Bible that is the subject of that study.

When biblical writers utilized a particular literary form, they intended for it to have a specific effect on their audience. This concept can be understood by examining genres that are familiar to us in our contemporary setting. For example, novels that are comedies inspire good and happy feelings in their readers; tragedies, on the other hand, are meant to induce sorrow. What is true of the intended effect of literary forms in contemporary literature is also true of literary forms found in the Bible.

THE BOOK OF DANIEL

The book of Daniel is one of the most beloved books of the Old Testament. Perhaps no other book is filled with as many memorable stories about ordinary people overcoming danger and persecution while remaining faithful to God. Yet there is a considerable cultural chasm between the modern reader and the book of Daniel. We are too far removed from harems, kings, and ancient court intrigues to fully understand and appreciate these stories.

The latter half of Daniel is even further removed from the modern reader. While the first half of the book contains popular stories we know and love, the latter half is filled with unfamiliar imagery and predictions about events in a world we do not understand. Though many people approach this book with the belief that it prophesies the future, it is far more fruitful to analyze Daniel in the context of apocalyptic literature. A renewed appreciation for history, context, and literary style is important for any student of Scripture, and especially for the reader of such a rich and intriguing book as Daniel.

As we read Daniel, there is a barrier we must overcome. While this barrier exists in any biblical text, it is perhaps more pronounced in Daniel than in any other Old Testament book. Most Western Christians live in powerful nations in which comfort and wealth are a given. But for the first readers of Daniel, hardships and political oppression were a daily reality. The ancient Jews had very little control over any aspect of their lives. In order to understand these stories, we must enter their world of oppression and stark political imbalance. While this might be a difficult task for us, it is necessary. Even if our personal circumstances differ from those of the characters in this text, the book of Daniel has theological significance for modern Christians.

Another barrier in our reading is the idea that Daniel predicts the future. As a result, many modern readers pore over details in Daniel, searching for clues that point to modern political identities. However, this is not how Daniel or other ancient prophetic books functioned. While this book does not predict the future, it does give the modern reader confidence that God will ultimately triumph.

Who Wrote Daniel?

One of the first problems a modern reader confronts in this book is the author's identity. Traditionally, the author has been identified as Daniel—however, that view has been seriously challenged for some time. The main evidence for Daniel as the author is the fact that Daniel's visions are described from a first-person perspective in chapters 7–12. Although this fact ends the conversation for some people, this view is not without its problems: the first six chapters of Daniel are written in the third person. What is a reader to make of this split between the first- and third-person perspectives?

Who is this Daniel our text describes? There may have been a Daniel who existed during the time of the Babylonian exile and around whom these heroic stories sprung up. If that is the case, we know nothing more about him. There are other instances of the name in the Old Testament, but these seem to refer to an ancient Daniel, not this hero who is faithful during the exile. In Ezekiel 14:14, the prophet refers to Noah, Daniel, and Job. Noah and Job are people from Israel's distant past and would hardly be contemporaries of Daniel. This instance of the name is also spelled differently and would be better rendered Danel.

There is another problem with the theory that this book was written by a single author: half of Daniel is written in Aramaic, while the other half is written in Hebrew. More precisely, chapters 2–7 are written in Aramaic, and chapters 1 and 8–12 are written in Hebrew. Most of the familiar stories about Daniel and his three friends are written in Aramaic; the introduction to the book and the strange visions of the latter half are written in Hebrew. Chapter 7 is the only chapter that breaks this pattern: it is the first chapter that describes Daniel's visions, and it is written in Aramaic. We will address this anomaly in more detail later.

Why would a single author decide to write a literary work in two starkly different languages?

There are many possible explanations for this difference in language. However, the simplest explanation is that there are multiple authors. An author living in the time of the exile writes about Daniel and the other three faithful heroes in the third person; a later author then writes the last five chapters in Hebrew, in the first person. This second author incorporates the heroic stories from the exile into the apocalyptic sections in the latter half of the book. These two works are then combined into a single literary work: the book of Daniel that we have today.

The possibility of multiple authors bothers some people—they feel it undermines the veracity of the Bible. They believe that because Daniel is mentioned, he must be the sole author. In our modern conceptions of authorship, the involvement of another writer might seem fraudulent. However, it is vital that we not impose our modern perspectives on people who lived in a far different time and place than our own. The idea of copyrighted material was foreign in ancient times, and most works of literature were composed anonymously. Whole genres of literature were written in the names of prominent people, especially heroes from the past. This is particularly true of apocalyptic literature. Most scholars see the second half of Daniel as an early apocalyptic work, so ascribing these visions to Daniel would be an expected part of an apocalypse.

If the Daniel from the sixth century BCE is not the author of this book, then who is? It is impossible to trace this book back to any specific author. However, we can trace it to a group: it seems likely that the author would have been part of a group of faithful Jews living in a time of extreme duress. These Jews would have observed the traditions and laws of Judaism and would have been resistant to the encroaching influence of Hellenization. As they lived beneath another kingdom that sought to end their religious practices, the stories of Daniel and his friends gained a new importance for these Jews. Later, another author composed an apocalyptic work in Daniel's name and combined it with the earlier stories from the exile.

Historical Context

It is helpful to understand the time period we will reference throughout this study. The hero stories in chapters 1–6 are straightforward and powerful, but it is easy to get lost in the kings and kingdoms that are described. When we enter the book of Daniel, Nebuchadnezzar is a relatively new king of the Babylonian Empire. The Babylonians were the world power at the time and had destroyed Jerusalem in 586 BCE. As a result of this defeat, many Jews were deported to Babylon and forced to live there in exile.

Around the time of Israel's exile, the new Persian Empire adjacent to Babylon was expanding rapidly and becoming increasingly powerful. The last Babylonian king, Nabonidus, had provoked an internal crisis by leaving Babylon for ten years. In his absence, he appointed Belshazzar as co-regent. This absence sparked internal strife which in turn weakened the morale of the Babylonian people and army. While Belshazzar reigned, the end of Babylon came swiftly: in 539 BCE, the Persian army easily defeated the dispirited Babylonian army, and Cyrus, the Persian ruler, entered Babylon. This was a positive development for the Jews in exile—the Persians ruled with much greater sensitivity and autonomy than the Babylonians and allowed the first of the Jews to return to their homeland.

Persia ruled until 333 BCE, when Darius III and the Persian Empire were defeated by Alexander the Great, and the Greek Empire reached its widest sphere of influence. This conquest also began an era in which the Greek culture and philosophy began to influence the whole region, known as the period of Hellenization. A few years later, when Alexander the Great unexpectedly died in 323 BCE, the Greek Empire was suddenly divided into many parts. Alexander's kingdom was divided among different military leaders, all of whom had their own territorial ambitions. These rival leaders included the Ptolemaic rulers in Egypt and the Seleucids in what is now modern-day Syria. The Jews who had returned to Palestine were located directly between these competing factions of the former Greek Empire. These factions frequently went to war with each other, and Palestine was pressured from both sides.

Eventually, the Seleucids pushed back the Ptolemaic rulers and governed Palestine starting in 200 BCE. While the Seleucids were never nearly as powerful as the great kingdoms that came before them, they ruled more harshly and threatened the Jews' existence in the mid-second century BCE. Their oppressive rule ended in 164 BCE when the Jews rebelled and regained their independence from the Seleucids. This timeline will be important to keep in mind as we read Daniel.

Date

Along with differing perspectives on authorship, the reader is faced with further questions and considerations when it comes to dating the book of Daniel. It is helpful to discuss these questions in tandem with the book's authorship, since the date of Daniel's composition is intertwined with determining the book's author.

When it comes to assigning a date to the book of Daniel, there are only two possibilities: the sixth century or the second century BCE. If Daniel himself penned the book, then it was written in the sixth century BCE. If the book was written later, a date in the second century BCE seems likely.

There is another option that might satisfy adherents of both views: It is possible that the first half of Daniel was compiled during the Babylonian exile in the sixth century. Many scholars have noted that it is highly unlikely a Palestinian Jew would have written or collected a series of tales that describe an exilic setting—it is not likely that the struggles of exile would have concerned Jews living in Palestine. On the other hand, for the Jewish community living in exile, the struggles portrayed in Daniel were a matter of daily concern. Daniel 2, for example, describes the achievements of Jews in a foreign court and emphasizes the benefits of remaining faithful to God in a gentile land. This perfectly describes the situation of the Jews in Babylon. In this scenario, we imagine that a later author compiled the hero stories from Israel's earlier history alongside the content of the latter half of Daniel, which was a product of the second century BCE.

There is considerable evidence that favors a later author or editor. As we discussed earlier, one of the questions we encounter in Daniel considers why the latter half of the book is written in Hebrew. The use of Hebrew would match the prevailing zealotry of the Maccabean period, would be a way to reclaim some of Israel's great history, and would be a purer expression of their Jewishness. Another piece of evidence that supports second-century composition is the type of Hebrew that is used—it reflects the type of Hebrew used in the second temple period, which imported words and phrases gained after the exile. If the latter part of Daniel were written in the sixth century BCE, a reader would have expected an older form of Hebrew. All of these clues point toward a later composition.

Either way, the answer to whether the book was written in the sixth or second century BCE does not change how a reader interprets the great hero stories found in the first half of Daniel—in both periods, the Jews were tested by an existential crisis. In Babylon, the Jews found themselves in a modern culture with great wealth and influence—it would have been easy to become enthralled with the size and wealth of this unrivaled world power. The three young Jewish men in Daniel had the opportunity to adopt Babylonian customs in pursuit of becoming part of the ruling class. In this context, the first half of Daniel would have served as a reminder that those who remain faithful can also find success.

The second century exemplified a different type of threat: the Jews were under the control of the Seleucid Empire, which stretched from the Mediterranean coast, through Persia, to modern-day Afghanistan. The Seleucid Empire was one of four major sub-kingdoms left over after the breakup of the Greek Empire. The Seleucids were in frequent conflict with the Ptolemy kingdom in Egypt, and this conflict frequently flared throughout Palestine. In 168 BCE, Antiochus IV, the latest Seleucid on the throne, invaded Egypt, and his campaign was thoroughly defeated. Newly humiliated, Antiochus returned home only to discover that an insurrection had started in Jerusalem. These pesky Jews were difficult to rule, and they constantly appealed to their God instead of the proper ruling authorities. His answer to this problem was to plunder the temple, set up an image of Zeus on the altar, and outlaw the Jewish faith altogether. A modern Seleucid ruler would teach these Jews how to worship a modern, approved god.

The faithful Jews in Jerusalem now faced a serious threat to their lives. Should they worship the false idol in the temple, or remain loyal to the one true God of Israel? One can easily see the parallels between this dilemma and the decision the three young men faced with Nebuchadnezzar's statue in Daniel 3. Whether our time frame is the exile in Babylon or the later oppression of the Seleucids, the stories from the first half of Daniel resonate equally well. Moreover, these stories still resonate today. While most of us do not face a life-or-death decision before a pagan king, we are tempted to drift away from God to better follow a host of lower deities. Our deities may not be stone idols on an altar, but they demand just as much of our loyalty as the old idols did, and they are just as contrived.

It is fair to say that the date we assign to Daniel does make a difference in how we read the latter half of the book—and this is where the main point of contention exists. If Daniel was written in the sixth century, then most of the latter half of Daniel is not only predictive in nature, but spectacularly accurate as well. If it was written in the second century, the latter half of Daniel is history written from the perspective of people who have witnessed these events. Many scholars have noticed that the second half of Daniel resembles a form of literature that was rapidly developing during this period: apocalyptic literature. We will discuss the apocalyptic genre in more detail below.

Some Christians believe that God is somehow diminished if we claim a second-century author; these believers take comfort in the thought of a God who knows the precise details of future events and how they will unfold. But the issue is not that simple, as much as we might like it to be. Rather, there has been a divide in Christianity for centuries.

First, there are those who believe that God knows every detail of the future and every decision that will create that future—in other words, God knows and has ordained the future and decisions of every person who lives. Conversely, those on the other side of this divide believe that God has granted each person the ability to make decisions for themselves. Those of us in the Wesleyan/Arminian tradition adhere to the latter view. We should be very careful before choosing to embrace the other side of this debate— there is much that hangs in the balance.

Literary Form

One of the enduring questions of Daniel is this: how did it come to be in its present form? As we discussed before, Daniel is a composite book. The first half of the book contains stories of heroes told in the third person; the second half is written in Hebrew from a first-person perspective and describes mysterious visions that are foreign to a modern reader. The book of Daniel as it exists today, then, appears to be the product of an effort to combine two separate writings into one text. The question is whether this was done during the exile or sometime during the reign of Antiochus IV Epiphanes in the second century BCE.

The heroic tales in the first half of the book center around four young Jewish men named Daniel, Hananiah, Mishael, and Azariah, who were taken from Palestine and forced to relocate to Babylon. While in Babylon, these men were noticed for their appearance, intellect, and talent, and were selected to participate in training that would prepare them for service within the Babylonian Empire. The text even gives us their new Babylonian names in chapter 1: Daniel was given the name Belteshazzar, Hananiah was named Shadrach, Mishael was called Meshach, and Azariah was named Abednego. As we are given their Jewish and Babylonians identities in the book's opening lines, the structure of these narratives is revealed: these stories will show the reader which identity these young men will cultivate and claim.

The first half of Daniel reflects the stories that most Jewish and Christian believers hold dear. Believers in every era have turned to these stories for encouragement and inspiration in the face of hardships, difficult decisions, and cultures that threaten to pull them away from their faith. Likewise, the four heroes' bravery is a model for modern-day believers who face similar crises of faith.

As we read, we are confronted with the question of what to make of the second half of Daniel. After an awkward third-person introduction in 7:1, Daniel's visions are written from a first-person perspective. Those who uphold that Daniel himself is the author point to this first-person perspective as evidence for their argument—still, they must explain the need for a third-person introduction. Likewise, those who believe that a later author wrote this section of the book point to the third-person introduction as evidence—yet they must also account for the first-person narrative that follows. The origins of the book of Daniel are not easily explained and present many important questions that we must navigate. Even more important than these questions are the content of these latter chapters.

It is hard to read the Bible without taking apocalyptic literature into account—the book of Revelation is the biggest example, but it is not the only one. By the time of the New Testament's composition, apocalyptic literature was well established, and there are many examples of the genre found outside of the Bible.

Many people mistakenly believe that apocalyptic literature describes what will take place at the end of the world. However, this narrow definition does not capture the term's true meaning. The word "apocalypse" simply means "the revealing." When someone goes to a play and the curtain is pulled back, that is an apocalypse. Like theater, an apocalypse does not reveal the future but, rather, unveils what has been hidden.

An apocalypse is written during times of persecution and is meant to inspire hope within its readers. This type of literature developed during and after the exile, as the Jews were dominated by a series of world powers. Typically, an apocalypse features an important figure from a marginalized group being sent on a supernatural journey or receiving visions that communicate a larger message. Most apocalypses were ascribed to Jewish heroes. In Daniel, for example, the fact that the final chapters are written in the first person is not necessarily evidence that it was written by a person named Daniel—rather, such an attribution is a convention of the apocalyptic genre.

As one of our first and best examples of an apocalypse, the book of Daniel calls the reader to participate in the hero's journey and see that God is still at work. Therefore, we can be encouraged as we enter its pages.

Entering the Story

Part of the reason why the stories in Daniel are so popular is because the first six chapters are so accessible. When we read these stories, we enter the world of the underdog. It is easy for us to place ourselves in circumstances where everything seems to be stacked against us. We imagine that with the Lord's help, we can overcome just as these young Jewish men did. Their journey encourages us to stay faithful. However, if this is our only response to these stories, we do not fully comprehend them.

While the modern reader, especially in the West, tends to read these narratives from a highly personal standpoint, the author's perspective is collective: these stories of Daniel and his companions express the plight and frustration of a powerless minority group. The Jewish captives in Babylon have no power to control or alter their circumstances, and success seems contingent upon giving up their identity. There is much that hangs in the balance—success in Babylon might mean the death of the Jewish people and the failure of the God of Abraham.

The difference between the Jewish exiles and the Babylonians was much more than a racial or ethnic distinction—there was a huge power imbalance as well. Babylon was the world power at the time, and the Jews were a conquered backwater. The only reason these Jewish men were in Babylon was because the Babylonians took them against their will. Whatever standard of living the Jews had was because the Babylonians allowed it to happen. Babylon had everything, and the Jews had nothing.

Even though the events in Daniel happened over 2,000 years ago, there is one key way that we can relate to the characters and enter the story. The Jews have found themselves in a completely foreign world, but that world is not dark and foreboding—rather, Babylon was powerful, rich, and alluring. For Jews with the talent and opportunity, there was a clear path to comfort, wealth, and power—far more power than would have been available to them had they remained in Jerusalem. They were in Babylon against their will, but if they played their cards right, there were riches and status to be gained.

The problem seems to be that while power and comfort were available to the exiles, the price for these gains was the abandonment of their Jewish identity and the Jewish God. While no one likes to experience intense hardship, it is relatively easy to understand how people remain faithful during difficult times. The scenario in Daniel is a little different: What does it mean to stay faithful in times of tremendous opportunity?

Doesn't God want me to be rich? Doesn't God want me to represent my people in powerful positions? How far can a follower of God go to gain an influential position? Undoubtedly, many people would have celebrated their fellow Jews' rise to power, even if it meant cutting a few corners to get there. Most people would have understood that there was a religious price to pay.

The writer of Daniel has a different view. For the heroes in these stories, the goal is not positions of power, but continued faithfulness to God. These are not stories that always have a happy ending in view—rather, these stories demonstrate that faithfulness means taking risks. These heroes declare, "We will not eat the king's food, even if it means being removed from the leadership program. Even if God doesn't save us from burning today, we still will not bow down to your idols." Their story shows us that faithfulness is not always easy, and we can't always predict the consequences of standing up for our beliefs. Remarkably, the young heroes in Daniel gain success through their faithfulness and obedience, and they do not have to abandon their identity in the process. This is the main point of Daniel's early chapters, and it provides an opening for the modern reader to enter the story.

The latter half of Daniel remains more elusive for the modern reader. While the early chapters resonate with readers, the strange visions in the second half of the book are harder to navigate. How we treat these chapters determines our ability to enter the story. As we previously discussed, our dating of Daniel is an important consideration here: if Daniel wrote the latter half of the book in the sixth century BCE, then Daniel takes on the role of predictive prophecy. In that case, the reader does not enter the story at all, but merely observes the unfolding of a predetermined series of events.

If Daniel is apocalyptic, however, the reader will respond to the text differently. Apocalyptic literature is not futuristic, nor does it teach the reader about the end of the world. At its heart, apocalyptic literature is written by marginalized people in times of great persecution or hardship in an effort to provide hope and encouragement. Again, in apocalyptic stories, a well-known figure is taken on a supernatural journey in which events are revealed to the figure in order to bring hope to a community. Thus, apocalyptic literature does not reveal the future, but reveals present-day events in a new light in hopes that the revelation will result in a change of behavior. A modern example of this type of literature is Charles Dickens's *A Christmas Carol*. In the novella, the Ghost of Christmas Present appears to Scrooge and takes him on a journey to Bob Cratchit's home on Christmas Day. While there, Scrooge is able to see the family's modest belongings and the meager meal they share on this sacred holiday. The hope is that Scrooge will see how his meager pay has left the family in poverty, and later change his behavior as a result of his supernatural journey.

This is an important distinction when we read Daniel. If we read Daniel as predictive, the text becomes a historical puzzle to be solved—therefore, if we can decipher who the text addresses, we can determine the events that will take place. There are numerous presuppositions one must make in order to read the text in this way: First, the reader must believe that the predictions are specific and accurate. Then, they must believe that God has executed specific plans that cannot be altered. Lastly, the reader must believe that human freedom is not an active force in the world, but rather, events occur exactly as God planned beforehand.

Apocalyptic literature operates at a different level—again, it attempts to provide hope to a marginalized group. How does apocalyptic literature accomplish this? In our book, Daniel is the famous figure who is taken on a supernatural tour—in this case, he receives a vision. The kingdoms in this vision are described in terms of what is to come—however, the reader recognizes three of these kingdoms from the past. This leaves a fourth kingdom that we do not recognize as historical. While this may lead the modern reader to speculate about the kingdom's identity, the ancient reader would have taken away a different lesson: if God has overcome these three kingdoms throughout history and has preserved the Jews through it all, then he will surely overcome the fourth kingdom as well. Therefore, stay faithful to the God who overcomes all earthly kingdoms.

This is a message that still resonates today. We still serve a God who overcomes and blesses his people in the midst of hardship—we can have hope because God has done this in the past, and will still do it today.

Once again, some people are troubled because Daniel seems to be the self-identified author. They fear that the involvement of another author would lead to the conclusion that the Bible is unreliable. However, nothing could be further from the truth. Daniel is credited as the author not in an attempt to deceive readers, but in order to honor and emphasize the importance of these stories.

Some might ask more specifically why the authors chose to link Daniel to the apocalyptic visions in the latter half of the book. This leads to the more serious question of *why* a Jewish author (or authors) living in Palestine would choose to attach their apocalyptic writings to texts of an entirely different genre (Diaspora tales). The answer is that Daniel is the figure who speaks most meaningfully to their present situation—in the midst of the Jews' ongoing persecution by the Seleucids, the story of Daniel overcoming the Babylonians is profoundly resonant.

Context of the Book

As we previously discussed, there are two options for the timeframe of Daniel's composition. The good news is that regardless of which option we choose, the broad contextual events are remarkably similar: In both eras, the Jews are persecuted by greater powers, and their future as a distinctive people is threatened.

The earlier era, the sixth century BCE, is the far better known of the two options. In this era, after Nebuchadnezzar conquers Jerusalem, a large number of Jews (not all of the Jewish people, but the best and brightest among them) are taken to Babylon in captivity. When the modern reader hears the word "captivity," images of deprivation spring to mind. However, this is not the case in Babylon—the Jews' material circumstances are better in captivity than they would have been in Jerusalem. Babylon is more influential, more powerful, and certainly far wealthier than Palestine. The challenge for these prisoners is to remain faithful to God in a land that is far more comfortable and prosperous than the land they left behind.

There is another sixth-century event described in the first half of Daniel. Not long after the captives arrive in Babylon, the Persians defeat the Babylonians, and the Persian Empire rises to dominance. This is good news for the Jews, because the Persians are far more accommodating to weaker nations than the Babylonians were. Immediately, Cyrus (the Persian ruler) allows the Jews to slowly begin returning to their homeland. Two world-dominating powers tower within the first of half of Daniel, and the young Jews remain faithful through both.

There is universal agreement about the historical context of the heroic tales in Daniel's first half—the disagreement centers on the context of the second half. There are some who still hold that Daniel, or a contemporary of Daniel, is the author of the second half. However, the majority of scholars believe that the textual evidence supports a second-century author for the latter chapters. In the second century BCE, another power has risen, and the Jews are threatened again.

One of the divided portions of the Greek Empire, the Seleucid Empire, controls Palestine during this era. In 168 BCE, the Seleucids launch a disastrous military campaign in Egypt and are defeated. With this, the Seleucids' territorial ambitions are defeated, and in the wake of that loss, the Jews begin a revolt in Jerusalem. Still stinging from his Egyptian defeat, the ruler of the Seleucid Empire, Antiochus IV, decides to teach these rebellious Jews a lesson. From his perspective the problem is obvious: these uncivilized Jews do not worship the proper, accepted Greek gods, and their temple seems to be a focal point for this rebellion.

Thus, Antiochus IV decrees that the Jewish temple should be plundered and an image of Zeus erected on the altar. Once again, the distinctiveness of the Jewish people is at stake. How will the Jews survive and thrive if a foreign leader abolishes the worship of God and forces the people into worship of false gods? The situation is different, but it is the same old problem that the Jews faced in exile.

One of the major questions Daniel evokes regards the identity of the kingdoms represented by the statue in chapter 2 and the beasts in chapter 7. There are four major parts of the statue: the head, constructed from gold; the chest, made of silver;

the thighs, fashioned from bronze; and the legs and feet, made of iron and clay. Most scholars assert that the head represents the Babylonians, the chest represents the Medes, the bronze thighs represent the Persians, and the legs and feet represent the remaining Greek kingdoms of the Seleucids and Ptolemies. No other combination seems to fit. The same empires are in view in the beast imagery of Daniel 7. The prevailing interpretation is that these beasts represent (in order) Babylon, Persia, Greek, and finally Rome. But this interpretation has problems: First, Persia cannot be described as inferior to Babylon in any way—rather, this is an obvious description of the Medes. The primary motivation behind the prevailing theory is for Rome to be the fourth kingdom, an interpretation that stems from modern interpretive desire more so than a sound hermeneutic. We must remember the first readers' perspective: while the Seleucid Empire is by far the weakest of the empires described, it is also the problem that presently looms over the Jews and which compromised the temple. From this perspective, their immediate presence and power over the temple would make the Seleucids a threatening power.

There is one more thing to say about those who want to make Daniel into a predictive prophecy: Chapter 11 does not read like any predictive literature. Rather, its rich historical details make it read like a history book or a journalistic account from second-century Palestine—its details match events that occurred in this time and during this period. For these reasons, it is hard to imagine this section emerging from any period besides the second century BCE—that is, until verse 40. When we hit verse 40, the historical description stops, and the events that are described simply do not and did not happen. This may reflect the author's attempt at prediction, including the fact that—like most attempts at specific predictive literature—it failed since these events never happened.

Some commentators try to argue that in chapter 11, Daniel skips forward to a description of the future antichrist—some theological circles uphold this view today. However, this interpretation is likely incorrect for two reasons: First, it is difficult to imagine that the writer goes into great detail about second- and third-century kings only to abruptly jump to descriptions of a vague future that readers cannot envision. Second, neither the concept nor the title of "antichrist" is introduced until some 250 years later, in 1 John. The author of Daniel cannot be referring to a concept that does not yet exist in any other literature.

The theme of Daniel is a question: how will the Jews survive as a people? As these stories move through a series of leaders, we see that God is sovereign over the Babylonians as well as their Persian successors. Throughout the years, many have attempted to identify the kingdoms represented in the visions described in the book of Daniel. Some argue that these visions do not represent a sequence of kingdoms, but rather a composite of all kingdoms that stand against God and lead his people astray. When the rock smashes the statue in Nebuchadnezzar's dream, it symbolizes that Daniel and his friends would rather die than worship at the altar of any earthly kingdom.

The First Readers

The first readers of Daniel lived in a far different world than ours. As a result, it is difficult for us to enter their story. We have discussed the possibility that Daniel was written in either the sixth or second centuries BCE. In either century, the first readers lived in oppressive conditions. The nations around them were large and powerful, and the Jews did not control their own destiny—they were either in captivity or under foreign occupation. Daniel was written in response to that feeling of powerlessness.

The problem for the modern reader is this: we cannot imagine their plight. Babylon and Persia were unrivaled as world powers. We struggle with Daniel because we live in the modern Babylon. This is not a moral judgment, but a simple observation of the power of Western Europe or North America. While we are used to voting and pursuing careers of our own choosing, Daniel and his contemporaries had no comparable opportunities. They were in Babylon because they were captured in a military invasion, and they had access to specialized training only because they were selected by their captors. Their lives, their safety, and their faith hung in the balance, and the threat was very real.

Yet there are times when we too face hardship and persecution—and this is where most readers will appreciate Daniel. As we read about Daniel's response, we are emboldened to be faithful. There are also times when we wonder if our own faith will survive. This is the point at which the apocalyptic sections are valuable—apocalyptic literature assumes that faith hangs in the balance. If Daniel merely reveals a future that is set in stone, we cease to be actors in our own world—instead, we simply observe the events that God has set in motion. The second half of Daniel calls us to remember that God has acted on his people's behalf in the past. When we remember, we know that God is still working in this way. While God is not surprised by any of humanity's actions, the exact events are not fixed. We are also reminded that God's kingdom will prevail. This fact gives us courage to stay faithful to the true God and not the false idols of kingdoms that will crumble and fall away.

Major Theological Themes

The narratives and apocalyptic visions in the book of Daniel come together to illustrate several key theological themes:

 The kingdoms of this world are corrupt. We live in a world where earthly kingdoms still wield great power, and where we often encounter evil. These kingdoms often act in unjust ways.

 False gods threaten to lead us astray. We are not immune to the influence of false gods in our time—false gods can be literal idols, but they can be other things as well. Both in ancient times and today, power, wealth, and popularity can lead us away from God.

 God is sovereign. There are times when it seems that earthly powers and kingdoms have all the power. But God is not surprised or threatened by these powers, and he still has supreme authority over them all.

 Idolatry and blasphemy lead to ruin. The worship of false gods and the use of sacred things for profane purposes results in the downfall of those who flout God's holiness.

 God distributes judgment and provides opportunities for repentance. God sees and will judge the actions of every earthly power. He honors those who repent—even those as selfish and proud as Nebuchadnezzar.

God calls us to obedience and faithfulness. We are called to be faithful, even in times of great difficulty. In doing so, we honor God—and God honors those who remain faithful.

 Obedience leads to success. God offers us opportunities to find success in the world around us by remaining faithful and obedient to him and his commands.

 We will face persecution. In this world, persecution is both expected and constant. However, persecution will never have the last word when it comes to God's people.

 God is powerful. While overt divine intervention is not guaranteed to us, God can show up and do miraculous things in the midst of our circumstances.

 God's kingdom is coming. We should not trust in worldly kingdoms, because eventually, they will all fail. Instead, we should place our faith in the coming kingdom of God.

Timeline for the Study of Daniel

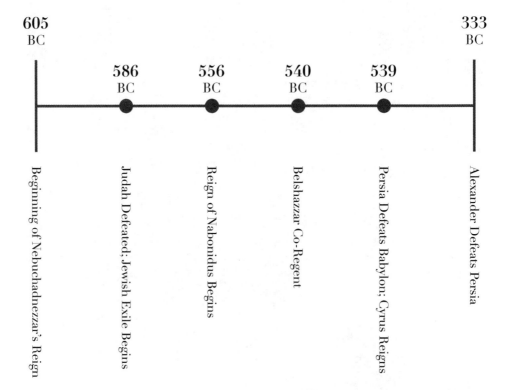

605 BC — Beginning of Nebuchadnezzar's Reign

586 BC — Judah Defeated; Jewish Exile Begins

556 BC — Reign of Nabonidus Begins

540 BC — Belshazzar Co-Regent

539 BC — Persia Defeats Babylon; Cyrus Reigns

333 BC — Alexander Defeats Persia

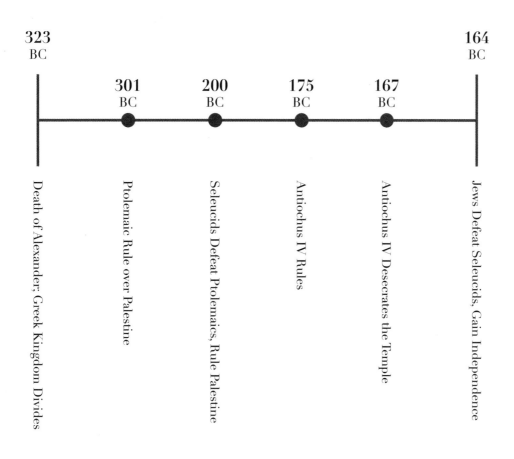

323 BC — Death of Alexander; Greek Kingdom Divides

301 BC — Ptolemaic Rule over Palestine

200 BC — Seleucids Defeat Ptolemaics, Rule Palestine

175 BC — Antiochus IV Rules

167 BC — Antiochus IV Desecrates the Temple

164 BC — Jews Defeat Seleucids, Gain Independence

23

DANIEL 1

This introductory chapter is a story about a foreign palace court and is political in nature: Those in power will give these young men a chance at political advancement if they assume the practices and identity of Babylonian culture. The modern reader often fails to appreciate the opportunity these young men have—they are captives, but have the chance to be part of the ruling class of the foremost world power. All they need to do is adopt Babylonian customs. Which will these young men choose: faithfulness to God, or loyalty to a powerful, wealthy kingdom?

WEEK 1, DAY 1

Listen to the story in Daniel 1 by reading it aloud several times until you become familiar with its verses, words, and phrases. Enjoy the experience of imagining the story in your mind, picturing each event as it unfolds.

WEEK 1, DAY 2

DANIEL 1

The Setting

This is the story that sets the stage for the rest of Daniel. Here we learn that the Jews are not in control of their own political fortunes and are exiles in the foreign land of Babylon. The king chooses four of the best of the Jewish youth for their talent and potential, and begins training them for future leadership positions.

The Plot

This is fundamentally a story about identity. The author purposefully gives the reader both of the Jewish men's names: their Hebrew names, and their Babylonian names. This subtly raises the question of which identity these young men will choose.

Some people read this chapter as a set of dietary guidelines, as if the issue were one of calories. The ancient reader, however, would have been aware of the Jewish food laws in the background of this narrative. Thus, the issue at stake here is faithfulness to Judaism. For the young men in our story, eating meat from the king's table would have meant abandoning their Jewish identity. Which identity will they choose, and what will be the result of that choice? There are communal consequences that hang in the balance.

To discover the plot of Daniel 1, let's examine the passage by dividing it into six sections. **Below, summarize or paraphrase the general message or theme of each grouping of verses (following the pattern provided for verses 1–2 and 3–5).**

1. Daniel 1:1–2

Nebuchadnezzar, the king of Babylon, besieges Jerusalem and plunders the Jewish temple.

_____

_____

2. Daniel 1:3–5

Nebuchadnezzar brings some exemplary young Jewish men to his court to be trained for service.

Meanwhile, he feeds them from his table.

_____

3. Daniel 1:6–7

_____

_____

_____

_____

_____

_____

4. Daniel 1:8–14

_____

_____

_____

_____

_____

_____

5. Daniel 1:15–17

_____

_____

_____

_____

_____

_____

6. Daniel 1:18–21

_____

_____

_____

_____

_____

_____

WEEK 1, DAY 3

What's Happening in the Story?

As we notice certain circumstances in the story, we will begin to see how they are similar to or different from the realities of our world. The story will become the lens through which we see the world in which we live today. In our study today, you may encounter words and/or phrases that are unfamiliar to you. Some of the particular words and translation choices for them have been explained in more detail in the **Word Study Notes**. If you are interested in even more help or detail, you can supplement this study with a Bible dictionary or other Bible study resource.

1. Daniel 1:1–2

These opening verses tell us that Nebuchadnezzar removes some articles from the temple in Jerusalem and takes them back to Babylon, where he places them in a temple to the Babylonian gods. While the modern reader might interpret this as either simple theft or the collection of wartime spoils, the ancient reader knew that the stakes were much higher—Nebuchadnezzar's plundering of the temple immediately puts him at odds with the God of Israel.

2. Daniel 1:3–5

Why train these Hebrew youth? At one point, Babylon tried to control Palestine without actually taking it over. The idea was that these capable young men—who were selected for their talent, appearance, and intellect[1]—would be influenced by Babylon's wealth and culture and become assets for the Babylonian Empire. Then, after their training, these men could work as liaisons or return to their homeland to help govern Palestinian affairs for Babylon.

_____

_____

_____

28

WORD STUDY NOTES #2

[1] There is considerable evidence that these young men were employed as eunuchs. At one point in his writings, the ancient Jewish historian Josephus mentions that young men were made eunuchs in order to serve in foreign courts. While Josephus does not specify which young men he is referring to, there is a distinct possibility that this description applies to Daniel and his friends. The notion that these men were eunuchs was also common in Rabbinic literature. If this is true, it would fulfill the words of Isaiah 39:7: "they will become eunuchs in the palace of the king of Babylon."

3. Daniel 1:6–7

One of this story's prominent features is that the young men are given new names in Babylon. Hebrew names carried great significance for the Jewish people, often describing them in relationship to God. In order to survive in exile, these young men would have to form new allegiances to Babylon and its gods, and these new names were meant to prompt the men to adopt new identities. It is not entirely clear why Daniel proceeds to tell the story using their Babylonian names rather than their Hebrew names—perhaps this detail is meant to highlight the alienation these men felt in a foreign land.

4. Daniel 1:8–14

The majority of this chapter describes the men's response to being offered food from the king's table. We do not know why their resistance begins here. They seem to have accepted their new names and entry into a foreign educational system—but for some reason, they draw a line when it came to food. There is a clue in the text: The writer states that they choose not to "defile" themselves with this food.[1] It seems that the young men decide to keep the kosher food laws. Eating unclean meat is a part of Babylonian identity that they cannot accept. Some commentators note a political motivation for abstinence from Babylonian food: If the men succeed in their new roles in the Babylonian court, the gods of Babylon will get credit for their success. But this is not acceptable—their God must receive the credit for their achievements. The author further indicates the men's loyalty to the God of Israel by using their Hebrew names during their ten-day trial period of refusing Babylonian food. The friends' refusal to eat the king's food is a subtle but clear rejection of Babylonian identity—they may be in Babylon, but they will never be of Babylon.

WORD STUDY NOTES #4

[1] This language does not mean that Daniel was motivated by ascetic concerns—later, in Daniel 10:3, it is clear that the men have no trouble eating meat when it does not come from the king's table. The word "defile" refers to impurity in a religious or ceremonial context. Thus, Daniel avoids the meat because he fears it is unclean according to Jewish law.

5. Daniel 1:15–17

It is important that we do not miss the point of this story. The message is not that vegetarians are healthier than those who eat meat; nor is it that those who avoid pork are superior to those who eat it. The point here is that the men's condition is not the outcome that the average reader would expect—Daniel and his friends should not have been healthier than the other men, but they were. Thus, divine intervention is assumed: the only explanation for this unexpected outcome is God's involvement.[1]

6. Daniel 1:18–21

Eventually, the four friends are rewarded for their faithfulness to keeping kosher. While they still remain in the Babylonian court system, their success is a victory for the God of Israel and a testimony that obedience is worth it. This would have comforted the early readers of Daniel, especially those who were in the midst of persecution. This is the central message of the book of Daniel. Thus, this story is a great introduction to the rest of the book.

_____

_____

_____

_____

_____

_____

_____

_____

_____

_____

_____

_____

_____

_____

_____

_____

WEEK 1, DAY 4

Obedience in Exile and the Story of God

Whenever we read a biblical text, it is important to ask how the text we are reading relates to the rest of the Bible. This is not the only place in the Bible where obedience to God enables oppressed people to overcome their trials. **In the space provided below, write a short summary of how the theme of faithfulness in the midst of trials is demonstrated elsewhere in Scripture.**

1. Judges 7:7–9, 17–21

_____

_____

_____

_____

_____

_____

_____

_____

2. 1 Samuel 17:45–51

_____

_____

_____

_____

_____

_____

_____

_____

_____

If you have a study Bible, it may have references in a margin, a middle column, or footnotes that point to other biblical texts. You may find it helpful in understanding how the whole story of God ties together to look up some of those other scriptures from time to time.

3. 1 Kings 18:22–39

_____
_____
_____
_____
_____
_____
_____
_____
_____
_____

4. Acts 12:5–11

_____
_____
_____
_____
_____
_____
_____

5. Acts 16:25–35

_____
_____
_____
_____
_____
_____
_____

WEEK 1, DAY 5

Daniel and Our World Today

When we enter into the intriguing narrative of Daniel 1, the story becomes the lens through which we see ourselves, our world, and God's action in our world today.

Answer these questions about how we understand ourselves, our world, and God's action in our world today.

1. This is a story about being tempted by a wealthier and more powerful culture than one's own. In what ways do power and money tempt Christians today?

_____

_____

_____

_____

_____

_____

_____

_____

_____

2. What is more dangerous for a believer's spiritual health: hardship and struggle, or wealth and ease? Why?

_____

_____

_____

_____

_____

_____

_____

_____

_____

3. In what other areas of modern life are Christians tempted to find their identity? Why are we so quick to surrender our identity?

_____

_____

_____

_____

_____

_____

_____

_____

4. It's surprising when Daniel and his friends emerge healthier after their dietary test. In what surprising ways are faithful Christians better off today?

_____

_____

_____

_____

_____

_____

_____

5. The young men in our story find success because of their obedience. In what ways can modern Christians demonstrate obedience?

_____

_____

_____

_____

_____

_____

Invitation and Response

God's Word always invites a response. Think about the way the theme of obedience in exile speaks to us today. How does it invite us to respond?

The text invites us to follow the example of Daniel and his friends-it spurs us to seek success through faithfulness rather than conformity; to stand firm in our convictions; and to give God the glory for our accomplishments.

What is your evaluation of yourself based on any or all of the verses found in Daniel 1?

DANIEL 2

Imagine being one of the first readers of this story: You are part of a marginalized group that is suffering under the power of Babylon or the Seleucids. Then the king summons a young man from your powerless community in order to put him to the test. The stakes are high as Daniel steps forward to represent you, your faith, and your God. Will Daniel show himself to be wiser than all of the king's other advisors?

WEEK 2, DAY 1

Listen to the story in Daniel 2 by reading it aloud several times until you become familiar with its verses, words, and phrases. Enjoy the experience of imagining the story in your mind, picturing each event as it unfolds.

WEEK 2, DAY 2

DANIEL 2

The Setting

As chapter 2 begins, the focus shifts to the palace court and to Nebuchadnezzar, the king of Babylon. The king has a strange dream and is unable to find anyone who can tell him what it means. This is where Daniel enters the scene.

This story should feel familiar to us, as it is a story we've read previously in the Old Testament: In Genesis 41, we read about another foreign king who was troubled by a dream. In that story, the king summons Joseph, and God enables Joseph to interpret the king's dream. In Daniel 2, the question is whether another young Jew will be able to demonstrate God's wisdom in a foreign land.

The Plot

To discover the plot of Daniel 2, let's examine the passage by dividing it into eight sections. **Below, summarize or paraphrase the general message or theme of each grouping of verses (following the pattern provided for verses 1–3 and 4–13).**

1. Daniel 2:1–3

Nebuchadnezzar is plagued by disturbing dreams and calls in his advisors to interpret for him.

_____

_____

_____

_____

2. Daniel 2:4–13

When he finds that his advisors can neither describe nor interpret his dream, Nebuchadnezzar becomes enraged and orders that all his wise men be executed.

_____

_____

_____

_____

3. Daniel 2:14–16

4. Daniel 2:17–23

5. Daniel 2:24–30

6. Daniel 2:31–35

_____
_____
_____
_____
_____
_____
_____
_____
_____
_____

7. Daniel 2:36–45

_____
_____
_____
_____
_____
_____
_____
_____
_____

8. Daniel 2:46–49

_____
_____
_____
_____
_____
_____
_____
_____
_____
_____

WEEK 2, DAY 3

What's Happening in the Story?

As we notice certain circumstances in the story, we will begin to
see how they are similar to or different from the realities of our
world. The story will become the lens through which we see the
world in which we live today. In our study today, you may encounter words and/or phrases that are unfamiliar to you. Some of
the particular words and translation choices for them have been
explained in more detail in the **Word Study Notes**. If you are
interested in even more help or detail, you can supplement this
study with a Bible dictionary or other Bible study resource.

1. Daniel 2:1–3

There is a new king in Babylon, and he has a disturbing problem: he is having dreams that are causing him to lose sleep. In
the ancient world, dreams were often viewed as a window of
communication with the gods. A recurring dream without interpretation would have been perceived as deeply troubling—especially for a new king in the second year of his rule. The dream
might contain bad news for the king, so it is important that he
find someone to decipher its meaning.

2. Daniel 2:4–13

The problem here is twofold: The king has a dream that needs
interpretation, and it seems no one can provide that interpretation. The issue is especially pressing for the wise men who serve
in the king's court—their lives are on the line as they remain sty-
mied by the dream.[1] The events here are a purposeful retelling of
Joseph's story from Genesis: While being forced to serve under
a foreign king, a young man is able to interpret a strange dream
for the ruler, and as a result of this God-given talent, the young
man succeeds and is given great responsibility. This sequence of
events becomes a template for how to succeed in a foreign land:
whether that foreign land is Egypt or Babylon, a Jew can flourish
through faithfulness and obedience to the almighty God.

41

WORD STUDY NOTES #2

[1] There is an interesting
literary device used in
verse 4: The first chapter
of Daniel is written in
Hebrew, but in verse 4,
when the astrologers
answer the king in
Aramaic, the language of
the entire story switches
to Aramaic and remains so
through chapter 7.

3. Daniel 2:14–16

While we do not know Daniel's exact role in Babylon, it is clear that Daniel has completed the training he started in chapter 1 and is considered one of the king's wise men. Unfortunately, this means Daniel is now facing the death penalty too. The reader does not know whether Daniel acts out of fear, political opportunism, or pure trust in God—but whatever his motivation, Daniel asks the king for time to properly interpret his dream.

4. Daniel 2:17–23

Daniel's character is revealed in this passage. We should remember that Babylon is oppressing the Jews and is considered their enemy. When Daniel learns of the king's problem and of the death penalty for those who could not interpret the dream, Daniel pleads for mercy; he pleads that the Jews' enemies might be spared. We might expect Daniel to plead only for the lives of the Jews, but instead, he prays for everyone involved.

Daniel then prays for wisdom. The author emphasizes that all wisdom comes from God—not even the wisest of men can rival the Lord. Daniel's God-given wisdom is demonstrated in the fact that he is concerned not only for himself, but also for the other men sentenced to death. The author purposefully contrasts his character with that of the foreign king: While the king acts out of bloodthirsty anger, Daniel cares for even the Babylonians.

5. Daniel 2:24–30

This section also shows Daniel's character. When he finally gets face-to-face with the king, Daniel gives God the credit for his abilities. He also tells the king that he was given the interpretation so that the king would have peace of mind—thus, the interpretation is framed in a way that shows concern for the oppressive king.[1] God's sovereignty is a key emphasis in this passage. The text does not suggest that God has pre-planned humanity's every action, but that God is neither overcome nor thrown off balance by any person's actions—even if that person is a powerful king. These verses also contain another powerful message which would have been scandalous at this time: that God loves Nebuchadnezzar too, and can use even a selfish, prideful king to accomplish his purposes.

42

WORD STUDY NOTES #5

[1] We see proper court protocol demonstrated in this palace encounter. Arioch introduces Daniel as though he has found him, stating, "I have found a man . . ." before bringing Daniel to the king. Daniel announces that the dream has to do with the future. He then describes what the king saw in his dream: a giant statue made of different metals. We see the symbolic use of metals in other ancient Greek and Zoroastrian texts, which sometimes used these metals to represent different kingdoms. Thus, the symbolism Daniel describes is not new and would have been familiar and accepted language for the time.

6. Daniel 2:31–35

This section of Daniel has garnered more speculation than any other part of the book. For generations, readers have tried to identify the various kingdoms represented in the description of the dream.[1] However, such speculation often obscures the larger intent of the story—this is particularly true if we read Daniel as predictive literature. It is dangerous to read too much into the text. The simplest explanation here is that there will be a succession of gentile kingdoms, but the God of Israel is more powerful and lasting than any of them. This would be wonderful news for the people oppressed by these kingdoms. The overall message for believers is to remain faithful to the God who is sovereign above all earthly kingdoms.

7. Daniel 2:36–45

Daniel makes no attempt to diminish Nebuchadnezzar's power or position—rather, he calls them the king of kings. But more importantly, Daniel informs the king that he only has power because the one true God has granted him that power. Readers who live in a powerful nation cannot grasp how powerful that statement is. Yet, if we imagine reading those words while living under constant oppression, we can see that this is a profound statement about the world: If God has more authority than Nebuchadnezzar, there is nothing to fear from oppressive rulers. Daniel does not stop there—he also describes a kingdom that is better and more just than any earthly nation. Notice in verse 44 that Daniel says this kingdom will arise "in the time of those kings." This is not a promise about what will happen after all earthly kingdoms come and go—it is a promise that God will build his kingdom in the midst of these others.

8. Daniel 2:46–49

At the end of this chapter, we return to the theme expressed in chapter 1: obedience and faithfulness result in ultimate success. We see that the wisdom of God's servants is far superior to that of the gentiles and their gods. The author emphasizes that those who have access to this wisdom have hope even in the direst of circumstances.

WORD STUDY NOTES #6

[1] There has been much written about the identity of the kingdoms represented in the dream, especially by those who believe that Daniel is predictive. But if we read Daniel historically, the simplest interpretation becomes clear: Babylon, as the text states, is the head of gold. The next kingdom, which is described as inferior, is the Medes. The third kingdom, one that will rule the whole earth, is the Persians, who succeeded the Babylonians. The identity of the fourth kingdom has been debated, but the text gives us clues: this fourth kingdom, which verse 41 describes as "divided," is a clear reference to the divided Greek kingdom. Two parts of that kingdom, the Seleucids and the Ptolemaics, inhabited either side of Palestine, and their battles spilled over into Palestine. Later, chapter 11 describes the events of the second and third centuries BCE in detail.

Those who engage in predictive speculations often find other identities for these kingdoms, which can oddly be made to fit the political situations present at the time the speculation is being made. A historical examination provides the most accurate answers to the text's descriptions and is the best way to identify these kingdoms. Still, these identities do not change the meaning of the text: God is greater than any earthly kingdom.

WEEK 2, DAY 4

The King's Dream and the Story of God

If you have a study Bible, it may have references in the margin, a middle column, or footnotes that point to other biblical texts. You may find it helpful in understanding how the whole story of God ties together to look up some of those other scriptures from time to time. Whenever we read a biblical text, it is important to ask how the text we are reading relates to the rest of the Bible.

This is not the only place in Scripture where we see a follower of God confronting a powerful ruler. **In the space provided below, write a short summary of how this theme from Daniel 2 appears in the other biblical passages.**

1. Genesis 41:14–40

_____

_____

_____

_____

_____

_____

_____

_____

2. Exodus 7:1–13

_____

_____

_____

_____

_____

_____

_____

_____

_____

3. John 18:28–40

4. Acts 26

WEEK 2, DAY 5

Daniel and Our World Today

When we enter into the intriguing narrative of Daniel 2, the story becomes the lens through which we see ourselves, our world, and God's action in our world today.

Answer these questions about how we understand ourselves, our world, and God's action in our world today.

1. The story of Nebuchadnezzar's dream is remarkably similar to the story of Joseph and the Pharaoh in Genesis. How would this similarity comfort the book's early readers as they experienced persecution?

_____

_____

_____

_____

_____

_____

_____

_____

2. Why would our author want to compare Daniel's compassionate concern with Nebuchadnezzar's bloodthirstiness?

_____

_____

_____

_____

_____

_____

_____

_____

_____

3. Instead of harsh language, Daniel uses kind words in speaking to Nebuchadnezzar—one might think that God cares for even the Babylonian king. How do you think the average Jew would perceive these kind words?

_____

_____

_____

_____

_____

_____

_____

4. One of this chapter's themes is that obedience to God leads to success. Is this still true today? When might this not be true?

_____

_____

_____

_____

_____

_____

_____

5. In verse 47, Nebuchadnezzar himself proclaims the Jewish God to be "the God of gods and the Lord of kings." How do these words have more impact coming from the Babylonian king?

_____

_____

_____

_____

_____

_____

_____

Invitation and Response

God's Word always invites a response. Think about the way the theme of success through faithfulness speaks to us today. How does it invite us to respond?

The story of Daniel's encounter with Nebuchadnezzar invites us to use our God-given abilities to demonstrate faithfulness, wisdom, and compassion to the world around us. It also reminds us that in doing so, we can make an impact that points people to God.

What is your evaluation of yourself based on any or all of the verses found in Daniel 2?

DANIEL 3

Something happens between the end of chapter 2 and the beginning of chapter 3—chapter 2 closes with Nebuchadnezzar recognizing the greatness of Daniel's God, but in chapter 3, he constructs a gigantic idol that he requires everyone to worship. The text does not tell us what causes this significant change in the king's outlook. Perhaps Nebuchadnezzar quickly forgets his encounter with Daniel, or perhaps he becomes so consumed with his own status and power that he willingly ignores Daniel's God.

This is a simple story about a test of wills. Will Shadrach, Meshach, and Abednego worship the image, or will they remain loyal to their God? The threat to their safety raises the stakes—we do not know how this struggle will end. There are two possible tragic outcomes for the young men: either they die for their choice to remain faithful; or, even more tragically, they abandon their God.

WEEK 3, DAY 1

Listen to the story in Daniel 3 by reading it aloud several times until you become familiar with its verses, words, and phrases. Enjoy the experience of imagining the story in your mind, picturing each event as it unfolds.

WEEK 3, DAY 2

DANIEL 3

The Setting

As the story begins, the image is constructed and the ruling officials gather to honor the idol. As the chapter unfolds, this scene becomes an intense, personal conflict with Daniel's contemporaries at the center. This is a political battle among a king, his golden image, and Israel's God.

The Plot

To discover the plot of Daniel 3, let's examine the passage by dividing it into seven sections. **Below, summarize or paraphrase the general message or theme of each grouping of verses (following the pattern provided for verses 1–6 and 7–12).**

1. Daniel 3:1–6

Nebuchadnezzar fashions a golden idol and orders all the nation's dignitaries to worship it. He institutes the death penalty for those who refuse.

2. Daniel 3:7–12

Some of Nebuchadnezzar's astrologers tell him that some of the Jews in his court (Shadrach, Meshach, and Abednego) are disrespecting him by refusing to worship the idol.

3. Daniel 3:13–15

4. Daniel 3:16–18

_____

_____

_____

_____

_____

_____

5. Daniel 3:19–23

_____

_____

_____

_____

_____

_____

6. Daniel 3:24–27

_____

_____

_____

_____

_____

_____

_____

7. Daniel 3:28–30

_____

_____

_____

_____

_____

WEEK 3, DAY 3

What's Happening in the Story?

As we notice certain circumstances in the story, we will begin to see how they are similar to or different from the realities of our world. The story will become the lens through which we see the world in which we live today. In our study today, you may encounter words and/or phrases that are unfamiliar to you. Some of the particular words and translation choices for them have been explained in more detail in the **Word Study Notes**. If you are interested in even more help or detail, you can supplement this study with a Bible dictionary or other Bible study resource.

1. Daniel 3:1–6

Nebuchadnezzar has shifted from honoring Daniel's God to threatening to kill Daniel for worshipping that same God. The modern reader does not fully appreciate the choice these young men were asked to make. This is not a simple question of worshipping either the Babylonian god or the Jewish God. The Babylonians were polytheists—from their perspective, these friends are simply being asked to add another god to their worship, not abandon their own. Yet for these Jewish men, there is no room for another God—they worship the one true God. We should also note that the image is made of gold. Perhaps this detail echoes Nebuchadnezzar's dream in which he was the head of gold and the statue bore the king's image.[1] While this is not explicitly stated, it seems like a reasonable connection to make. By listing all the officials who honored the statue, the writer builds tension and shows how isolated the young Jewish men were.

WORD STUDY NOTES #1

[1] The dimensions of the statue are startling: the author tells us that it is ninety feet tall. This would have made it among the largest ancient statues ever built. The only known statue that would rival this size is the famed Colossus of Rhodes. This detail about the statue's size serves to contrast Babylon's immense size and scope with the Jewish friends' relative powerlessness.

53

[1] Here we get a glimpse into the politics and intrigue of the palace court. The accusers turn the three friends' refusal to bow down into a personal offense: they tell the king that the men "pay no attention to *you*, Your Majesty . . . they neither serve *your* gods nor worship the image of gold *you* have set up." With the issue framed this way, the king's harsh reaction is thoroughly predictable.

2. Daniel 3:7–12

The tension in the story is heightened because we know the penalty for refusing to worship the idol: a gruesome death. Defying the king's orders would earn the offender the ultimate penalty. Verse 12 is filled with descriptive details that are easy to miss: first, the leaders who report the offense tell the king that "some Jews" will not bow down. This leads us to the inevitable conclusion that there are other Jews who do bow down—the temptation to follow the crowd is always strong. Moreover, a close reading of verse 12 indicates that the accusers' actions seem to be motivated by jealousy and political rivalry.[1] Notice that they describe the three men as those "whom you have set over the affairs of the province." Clearly, these accusers do not like the influence these Jewish men wield, and they want to take that influence for themselves.

3. Daniel 3:13–15

In these verses, the larger story narrows and becomes intensely personal: the king summons the three friends to stand before him as he gives them another chance. Musicians gather and strike up the music as the king commands the three friends to bow down before the image in his presence. As he does so, the king confidently asserts his absolute power: "what god will be able to rescue you from my hand?" One can imagine how early readers may have recalled what Psalm 2 says about earthly rulers: "The One enthroned in heaven laughs; the Lord scoffs at them."

4. Daniel 3:16–18

The three Jewish men stand alone and completely isolated before the king. Their response to the king's threats are perhaps the climax of the entire book and a wonderful illustration of faith. Their statement is one of hope more so than confidence as they calmly assert, "the God we serve is able to deliver us." This is not an example of blind faith—they admit that God may not rescue them from the king's sentence. Their faith is expressed not in the hope that God can save them, but in their loyalty that will be demonstrated either way. This uncertainty only adds to the tension in the story: Will God actually save them? Even the three friends do not know. Still, they make it clear that whatever the result, they will not bow to the culture's pressures and act unfaithfully.

5. Daniel 3:19–23

If the reader was hoping for a good outcome, the story takes a distressing turn in this section. The execution of Shadrach, Meshach, and Abednego is quickly carried out. The three friends' loyalty does not save them—instead, it only serves to intensify the king's fury. Their loyalty has only made their situation worse. The author adds more details here to build the tension: The king is filled with anger and orders the furnace to be heated to the maximum temperature. In fact, the furnace is so hot that it kills the soldiers tasked with throwing the three friends inside. The question here is clear: the furnace kills the best Babylonian soldiers, but what will it do to the faithful Jews?

6. Daniel 3:24–27

Nebuchadnezzar himself gives the answer to this question.[1] He looks in the furnace and exclaims, "I see four men walking around." The writer emphasizes the miraculous deliverance with further details: not only were the men unharmed in the fire, but their clothes didn't even smell like smoke. Through the execution Nebuchadnezzar ordered, God is showing the king who is really in charge. There has always been speculation about the fourth person in the furnace: Who was this fourth person? Was it God, or perhaps an angel? Again, we should be careful about such speculations. Furthermore, the identity of the fourth man does not make a difference in the story—whatever the case, it is still God who rescues the three men.

7. Daniel 3:28–30

This story ends triumphantly for the three men, and the king further promotes them. This demonstrates the rewards of continued faithfulness in the midst of persecution. The person who perseveres in obedience can hope to succeed, even if that success is not apparent in the present moment. This is an important lesson: most people seek success in life, but the story of these three friends reminds us that obedience comes before true success.

WORD STUDY NOTES #6

[1] It is difficult for the reader to visualize what is happening here. Some scholars suggest that the furnace in chapter 3 may be the same furnace that was used to make the golden image in the first place. In this case, there would have been an opening at the top where Shadrach, Meshach, and Abednego would have entered the furnace. It may have been built on a hill with an opening in the side of the furnace where the king could look into it.

WEEK 3, DAY 4

The Fiery Furnace and the Story of God

If you have a study Bible, it may have references in the margin, a middle column, or footnotes that point to other biblical texts. You may find it helpful in understanding how the whole story of God ties together to look up some of those other scriptures from time to time. Whenever we read a biblical text, it is important to ask how the text we are reading relates to the rest of the Bible.

This is not the only place in the Bible where God rescues those who were in danger because of their faithfulness. **In the space provided below, write a short summary of how the theme from Daniel 3 is demonstrated in the other biblical passages.**

1. 1 Samuel 17

_____

_____

_____

_____

_____

_____

_____

_____

2. Acts 4:13–22

_____

_____

_____

_____

_____

_____

_____

_____

3. Acts 12:1–11

4. Acts 16:25–34

5. Mark 16:1–8

WEEK 3, DAY 5

Daniel and Our World Today

When we enter into the intriguing narrative of Daniel 3, the story becomes the lens through which we see ourselves, our world, and God's action in our world today.

Answer these questions about how we understand ourselves, our world, and God's action in our world today.

1. It seems strange that Nebuchadnezzar would go from acknowledging the Jewish God's power to requiring the Jews (along with everyone else) to worship an idol. What would cause the king to make such a drastic turnaround?

_____

_____

_____

_____

_____

_____

_____

_____

2. Shadrach, Meshach, and Abednego were present with all the leaders of Babylon when they refused to bow down. Do you think the prominence of the people around them made it harder for them to resist? If so, in what ways?

_____

_____

_____

_____

_____

_____

_____

3. Which of the men's statements shows greater faith: their assertion that God could save them, or the statement that even if he didn't, they would still refuse to worship the idol?

_____

_____

_____

_____

_____

_____

_____

4. The story tells us that the king saw four men walking around in the fire, but it does not tell us who or what that fourth person was. Why do you think that is? How important is the answer?

_____

_____

_____

_____

_____

_____

_____

5. At the end of the story, Nebuchadnezzar exclaims that no God can save like the God of Shadrach, Meshach, and Abednego. Why was it important for the book's early readers to hear this from the Babylonian king?

_____

_____

_____

_____

_____

_____

Invitation and Response

God's Word always invites a response. Think about the way the theme of faith in the midst of trials speaks to us today. How does it invite us to respond?

This story invites us to follow Shadrach, Meshach, and Abednego's example by remaining loyal to God even when everyone around us is making compromises. It invites us to emulate their bold faith by remaining obedient regardless of whether God intervenes in our circumstances in the way we expect.

What is your evaluation of yourself based on any or all of the verses found in Daniel 3?

DANIEL 5

In this story, foreign rulers praise false gods and selfishly use holy items from the Jewish temple for their own profane purposes. The Babylonians commit a double sin here—blasphemy combined with idolatry. After flagrantly spiting God in this way, the new king, Belshazzar, calls on a lifeless statue to protect him from the consequences of his actions. Here we have another contest between the God of the Jews and the gods of the oppressors. We know which nation is more powerful, but which god is more powerful?

WEEK 4, DAY 1

Listen to the story in Daniel 5 by reading it aloud several times until you become familiar with its verses, words, and phrases. Enjoy the experience of imagining the story in your mind, picturing each event as it unfolds.

WEEK 4, DAY 2
DANIEL 5

The Setting

The setting in chapter 5 seems to be a large banquet. We know from extra-biblical sources that the Persians overthrew Babylon in a nighttime raid during a large banquet of Babylonian dignitaries (ancient records tell us this raid happened on October 12, 539 BCE). While we cannot prove it, it is highly plausible that the events described in chapter 5 depict the last night of the Babylonian Empire and that final banquet.

The Plot

We know from other Old Testament books that Israel's prophets are already proclaiming Babylon's downfall — perhaps Daniel too is quietly warning the new ruler of his imminent defeat. It is possible that the king is aware of these warnings and purposefully uses the items from the temple in a demonstration of his own power. This, of course, is a personal affront to the Jews.

To discover the plot of Daniel 5, let's examine the passage by dividing it into six sections. **Below, summarize or paraphrase the general message or theme of each grouping of verses (following the pattern provided for verses 1–4 and 5–9).**

1. Daniel 5:1–4

The new king Belshazzar uses goblets plundered from the Jewish temple in a banquet for his court. As they drink from the goblets, he and his guests praise false gods.

2. Daniel 5:5–9

In the midst of the king's banquet, a hand appears and writes a message on the wall. Belshazzar is shaken at the sight and commissions his wise men to interpret the writing, but none of them succeed.

3. Daniel 5:10–16

4. Daniel 5:17–21

5. Daniel 5:22–25

_____

_____

_____

_____

_____

_____

_____

_____

_____

_____

_____

_____

_____

_____

_____

6. Daniel 5:26–31

_____

_____

_____

_____

_____

_____

_____

_____

_____

_____

_____

_____

_____

_____

_____

WORD STUDY NOTES #1

[1] We have an important historical question to consider here: The Babylonians kept exhaustive records, and those documents contain no record of king named Belshazzar. This discrepancy has led many to believe that Belshazzar is little more than a figment of the ancient Jewish imagination. However, recent discoveries may call this conclusion into question—we now have evidence that Belshazzar was Nabonidus's son. Nabonidus was the last Babylonian king, and he left Babylon for a ten-year period near the end of his reign, during which he named Belshazzar co-regent. Belshazzar then ruled in Nabonidus's ten-year absence. It remains highly doubtful that Belshazzar was Nebuchadnezzar's son. But while this is almost certainly not true in a biological sense, that is probably not what the writer means— Belshazzar is not the biological descendant, but the political son of the previous king. There is a large time gap between the stories of chapters 2–4 and this story in chapter 5. While not all the questions about this text have been answered, there is historical corroboration for this chapter.

What's Happening in the Story?

As we notice certain circumstances in the story, we will begin to see how they are similar to or different from the realities of our world. The story will become the lens through which we see the world in which we live today. In our study today, you may encounter words and/or phrases that are unfamiliar to you. Some of the particular words and translation choices for them have been explained in more detail in the **Word Study Notes**. If you are interested in even more help or detail, you can supplement this study with a Bible dictionary or other Bible study resource.

1. Daniel 5:1–4

Our setting is once again the Babylonian court, only this time with a new king: Nebuchadnezzar's son.[1] This section also marks an obvious shift in tone. In earlier stories, Daniel seems favorably disposed toward Nebuchadnezzar; in chapter 5, however, he is happy to tell the new king of his impending doom. There is also a strong link between this story and the story in chapter 4: while the previous chapter focuses on Nebuchadnezzar's pride, this chapter focuses on Belshazzar's. In chapter 4, the father repents of his pride, but here we see that the son is unwilling to do so.

_____

_____

_____

_____

_____

_____

_____

_____

_____

_____

2. Daniel 5:5–9

This is another story in which God appears at the time we least expect, and in an unexpected way. In the middle of this story, a hand appears and starts writing on the wall.[1] While the reader knows that this is God's hand, to the polytheist king, there are a number of divinities who might be responsible for this hand. Whatever the case, it seems the king immediately recognizes the hand as a bad omen.

_____

_____

_____

_____

3. Daniel 5:10–12

There is a considerable time gap between the previous stories and this one—Daniel is now an old man. While the upstart new ruler might not know about Daniel and his past accomplishments, the queen (Nebuchadnezzar's wife), who is apparently still exerting influence behind the scenes, remembers Daniel's ability to interpret strange dreams and visions. Upon the queen's suggestion, the young, boastful king summons the elderly Daniel to the court.

Tensions are high as Daniel walks into the new ruler's presence. Belshazzar is young and perhaps unprepared for his new title and responsibility. He could not possibly measure up to the standards set by the great Nebuchadnezzar, the king Daniel remembered and had once served.

4. Daniel 5:13–17

There is a notable difference between the respect Nebuchadnezzar showed Daniel and the new king's rather abrupt manner—there is an undercurrent of disrespect in Belshazzar's greeting.[1] Daniel notices the slight and responds strongly—the reader can almost hear the aged Jew's annoyed tone as he answers the brash new king. In response to the perceived slight, Daniel refuses the king's offer of a reward. It is possible that Daniel refuses the reward out of pride, or perhaps Daniel has read the inscription on the wall and realizes the king has nothing to give.

WORD STUDY NOTES #2

[1] Daniel's early readers would have immediately recognized this as God's hand based on their knowledge of the rest of the Old Testament. For example, in Exodus 8:19, the Egyptians attribute the plagues to "the finger of God." Likewise, Exodus 31:18 states that the Ten Commandments were inscribed by "the finger of God." Psalm 8 tells us the heavens are the "work of [his] fingers." These references would have informed the ancient Jews' reading.

WORD STUDY NOTES #4

[1] When Daniel appeared before Nebuchadnezzar in previous encounters, the king honored Daniel—for example, in 4:9, he states, "I know that the spirit of the holy gods is in you." Conversely, Belshazzar treats Daniel with mockery. He seems to offer Daniel only faint praise in 5:16 when he says, "I have heard that you are able to give interpretations," and couches his promise of reward with the words, "if you can." This is a stark difference that most readers do not notice.

5. Daniel 5:18-28

In a role that has been assumed by many Jewish prophets before him, the aged Daniel confronts the king. The new ruler revels in his power and fails to recognize that there is a higher authority who judges even the most powerful gentile kings. Daniel condemns Belshazzar for his pride and tells him that the hand's writing on the wall serves to judge him.

_____

_____

_____

_____

_____

_____

_____

6. Daniel 5:29-31

In a confusing narrative twist, Daniel ultimately accepts Belshazzar's reward. The author does not tell us why. Perhaps Daniel accepts the reward because he knows it will be worthless in a matter of hours. We simply do not know. What we do know, however, is that the destruction of the Babylonian ruling class brings freedom for the Jews. Thus, the judgment described in Daniel has two contrasting consequences. While the kingdom's downfall was a tragedy for the Babylonians, for the Jews, it was a day that brought a reversal of fortunes. There is also a larger lesson in this story that begins with Belshazzar using items from the temple: there is a high price for profaning God.

_____

_____

_____

_____

_____

_____

_____

WEEK 4, DAY 4

The Writing on the Wall and the Story of God

If you have a study Bible, it may have references in the margin, a middle column, or footnotes that point to other biblical texts. You may find it helpful in understanding how the whole story of God ties together to look up some of those other scriptures from time to time. Whenever we read a biblical text, it is important to ask how the text we are reading relates to the rest of the Bible.

This is not the only place in Scripture in which God calls a prophet to confront a prideful king. **In the space provided below, write a short summary of how this theme from Daniel 5 is demonstrated in the other biblical passages.**

1. 1 Samuel 13

_____

_____

_____

_____

_____

_____

_____

_____

2. 2 Samuel 12

_____

_____

_____

_____

_____

_____

_____

_____

3. 1 Kings 18

_____
_____
_____
_____
_____
_____
_____
_____

4. Jeremiah 36

_____
_____
_____
_____
_____
_____
_____

5. Luke 3:1–20

_____
_____
_____
_____
_____
_____
_____
_____

WEEK 4, DAY 5

Daniel and Our World Today

When we enter into the intriguing narrative of Daniel 5, the story becomes the lens through which we see ourselves, our world, and God's action in our world today.

Answer these questions about how we understand ourselves, our world, and God's action in our world today.

1. Chapter 5 begins with the Babylonians using items taken from the temple in Jerusalem. What is the larger issue here: Babylonians using Jewish items, or people using holy items for profane purposes?

_____

_____

_____

_____

_____

_____

_____

_____

2. What are some holy things that we use in profane ways today?

_____

_____

_____

_____

_____

_____

_____

_____

_____

_____

3. What attitudes or traits led Belshazzar to be so unprepared for the judgment he would face?

_____

_____

_____

_____

_____

_____

4. In what ways do the rulers of our world refuse to recognize God? What are the consequences of this lack of recognition?

_____

_____

_____

_____

_____

5. What are some ways in which the church can help confront the rulers of our world?

_____

_____

_____

_____

_____

6. What are some more recent examples of events that meant downfall for some, and liberation for others?

_____

_____

_____

_____

Invitation and Response

God's Word always invites a response. Think about the way the themes of blasphemy, downfall, and liberation speak to us today. How do they invite us to respond?

This text reminds us to approach the holy God with fear and trembling. It invites us to
stand firm in the Spirit as we speak the truth to the power.

What is your evaluation of yourself based on any or all of the verses found in Daniel 5?

DANIEL 6

After the collapse of the Babylonian Empire, a new kingdom rules a vast swath of land that includes Palestine. Even with a new king on the throne, we have yet another story of internal political conflict. Some in the royal court are jealous of Daniel and his rise within the new ruling administration. These new political opponents plot to undermine Daniel by using his open worship of God against him. This chapter reinforces some of the key themes from previous chapters: namely, God still rules even when circumstances seem to indicate otherwise, and success is possible through faithfulness.

WEEK 5, DAY 1

Listen to the story in Daniel 6 by reading it aloud several times until you become familiar with its verses, words, and phrases. Enjoy the experience of imagining the story in your mind, picturing each event as it unfolds.

WEEK 5, DAY 2

DANIEL 6

The Setting

As we enter chapter 6, we should note that a new ruler has taken the throne (Darius the Mede), and a new empire is in control (Persia). This chapter also presents us with another historical problem: while the text tells us that the new king is named Darius, there was no one by that name who ruled Persia at or around that time. While there have been a few attempts to explain this discrepancy, none are completely satisfactory. For example, some scholars believe that Darius is a composite name for the first few rulers of the Persian Empire. Another intriguing possibility is that Darius and Cyrus are one and the same—"Darius" would have been the name his fellow Medes used, and "Cyrus" would have been the royal name by which he ruled the kingdom. For whatever reason, Daniel uses the Medes' name for this king. Whether these theories explain the name discrepancy or not, this detail has no impact on our interpretation: the issue here is not the ruler's name but how the ruler treats those who follow the Jewish God.

The Plot

To discover the plot of Daniel 6, let's examine the passage by dividing it into six sections. **Below, summarize or paraphrase the general message or theme of each grouping of verses (following the pattern provided for verses 1–5 and 6–9).**

1. Daniel 6:1–5

As the Persian king Darius assumes his rule in Babylon, he plans to appoint Daniel to a high political position. Upon learning this, Daniel's colleagues determine to undermine him.

_____

_____

2. Daniel 6:6–9

Daniel's enemies in the royal court convince Darius to decree that everyone must pray to the king alone for the next thirty days. Upon their suggestion, Darius sets the penalty for disobeying this edict: death by lions.

_____

_____

3. Daniel 6:10–14

_____

_____

_____

_____

_____

_____

4. Daniel 6:15–18

_____

_____

_____

_____

_____

_____

5. Daniel 6:19–23

_____

_____

_____

_____

_____

_____

6. Daniel 6:24–28

_____

_____

_____

_____

_____

_____

WEEK 5, DAY 3

What's Happening in the Story?

As we notice certain circumstances in the story, we will begin to see how they are similar to or different from the realities of our world. The story will become the lens through which we see the world in which we live today. In our study today, you may encounter words and/or phrases that are unfamiliar to you. Some of the particular words and translation choices for them have been explained in more detail in the **Word Study Notes**. If you are interested in even more help or detail, you can supplement this study with a Bible dictionary or other Bible study resource.

WORD STUDY NOTES #1

[1] The NIV translation "went as a group" does not capture the conspirators' attitude. The verb used here has meanings that range from "conspired" to "moved out of anger." In this case, the whole range of meanings apply—these men are plotting against God's faithful servant.

WORD STUDY NOTES #2

[1] Scholars have a difficult time verifying this edict against worshiping other gods—such a prohibition was out of character for the Persian rulers. It is possible that in the very early days of a new kingdom, recognizing the superiority of the Persian ruler would have been looked on favorably by the Persian gods. Making the new ruler the focus of the people's worship would have served to create allegiance to the new state.

1. Daniel 6:1-9

As we saw in chapter 5 when Daniel declined Belshazzar's initial offer of a reward, Daniel has served a number of kings, and never for selfish gain. His behavior has been spotless, and he has demonstrated integrity in every situation. Yet Daniel's integrity will not ensure his safety—his new opponents will seek to use his spotless behavior against him.[1]

2. Daniel 6:10

Unlike the previous public tests, this challenge is an intensely private struggle for Daniel. The question is this: who will be Daniel's god? Daniel could have quietly given up his daily practice of prayer—no one would have known if Daniel stopped praying in order to save his own life. This prohibition of private prayer seems like a strange edict and may reflect insecurity on the new leader's part.[1] It is not clear why a Persian ruler would issue such a religious edict, since the Persians were generally known for their leniency. Some believe this edict was meant to make the Persian king the nation's primary god. Others see a more benign, but no less serious attempt to declare the king the sole representative of the god(s). Either way, the edict demanded a level of allegiance that Daniel could not give.

3. Daniel 6:10–14

There is a stirring simplicity to this story that tells the reader a great deal about Daniel's character. The author tells us that Daniel prays three times each day. When it is time to pray, his usual practice is to retire to an upper room and pray with his windows open. These details are significant: the upper room tells us that Daniel is not making a spectacle of his prayer, and the open windows indicate that he is not hiding it either. Thus, Daniel does not flaunt the king's decree, but simply continues his normal religious practices. The aged Daniel continues living his life as he had before the decree was issued.

_____

_____

_____

4. Daniel 6:15–18

Seemingly trapped by his own decree, Darius follows through with the punishment for disobeying the law.[1] However, it is obvious that Darius's heart is not in this execution. The king also seems to hold onto a desperate hope that Daniel's God might save him from the lions. With this, the experienced Daniel confronts another generation and another ruler to demonstrate an important lesson once again: the true God can save from any world power. A modern reader might describe this scene as an execution, but it is more nuanced than that. This event is better described as an ancient "trial by ordeal." A trial by ordeal was a test that determined the fate of the accused. A person's death during the ordeal was considered proof of their guilt; survival was a sign of their innocence. Darius's actions are evidence of this sort of thinking: upon reaching the den the next morning, Darius calls out to Daniel in the hope he is still alive.

_____

_____

_____

_____

_____

_____

_____

WORD STUDY NOTES #4

[1] This passage portrays Persia's laws as harsh and inflexible, but this seems a little out of character given what we know about Persia. Still, such harshness was not unheard of: The last king of Persia, Darius III, would not change a death sentence once it was levied, and the ancient Code of Hammurabi states that it is a crime for a judge to alter a decision. It might also be said that in the ancient world, a king who often changed his mind would not have been considered authoritative or trustworthy. The descriptions in Daniel 6 seem consistent with these historical precedents.

5. Daniel 6:19–23

As the king rushes to the lion's den and calls out to Daniel, he expresses hope in Daniel's "living God." This language indicates that the king is impressed with the quality of Daniel's life. In saying that Daniel serves his living God "continually," the king also notes Daniel's faithfulness. When Daniel answers the king, we see that God has not only spared Daniel, but has made his rescue even more miraculous by preventing the lions from even touching Daniel's clothing. This is a God who saves completely.

_____

_____

_____

_____

_____

_____

_____

6. Daniel 6:24–28

At the end of chapter 6, we leave the foreign royal courts behind. In these stories, a series of rulers oppose Israel's God, and in each and every confrontation, God shows himself to be faithful and victorious over these rulers and their deities. The modern reader might think these stories are about heroic men—individuals confronting a powerful ruler against all odds. However, this thinking is a product of our individualistic culture. At their heart, these stories are about the Jews' survival as a distinct people, and the God of Israel's primacy over the false gods of powerful foreign kingdoms.

_____

_____

_____

_____

_____

_____

_____

_____

WEEK 5, DAY 4

The Lions' Den and the Story of God

If you have a study Bible, it may have references in the margin, a middle column, or footnotes that point to other biblical texts. You may find it helpful in understanding how the whole story of God ties together to look up some of those other scriptures from time to time. Whenever we read a biblical text, it is important to ask how the text we are reading relates to the rest of the Bible.

This is not the only place in Scripture where God transcends the natural world to help his people. **In the space provided below, write a short summary of how this theme from Daniel 6 is demonstrated in the other biblical passages.**

1. Exodus 13:17–14:31

_____

_____

_____

_____

_____

_____

_____

2. Jonah 1–2

_____

_____

_____

_____

_____

_____

_____

3. Matthew 14:22–33

_____

_____

_____

_____

_____

_____

_____

_____

_____

_____

_____

_____

4. Acts 16:16–34

_____

_____

_____

_____

_____

_____

_____

_____

_____

_____

_____

_____

WEEK 5, DAY 5

Daniel and Our World Today

When we enter into the intriguing narrative of Daniel 6, the story becomes the lens through which we see ourselves, our world, and God's action in our world today.

Answer these questions about how we understand ourselves, our world, and God's action in our world today.

1. In our own lives, we often expect God to protect us or deliver us from trouble. Daniel's conduct was above reproach, yet he was persecuted. How should this inform our expectations?

_____

_____

_____

_____

_____

_____

2. The conflict in Daniel 6 centers on Daniel's private worship practices. No one would have known if he changed his behavior. Why is it important that our private religious lives remain strong and consistent?

_____

_____

_____

_____

_____

_____

_____

_____

_____

_____

_____

3. Daniel neither grandstands about his religious life nor hides his loyalty to God. What lessons can modern believers learn from his behavior?

_____

_____

_____

_____

_____

_____

4. In these early chapters of Daniel, we see loyal Jewish men persevering through three different kings and two different kingdoms. Why is overcoming multiple rulers an important feature of these stories?

_____

_____

_____

_____

_____

_____

5. At the end of chapter 6, the foreign king praises Daniel's "living God," indicating that this God is both powerful and active. What would this message have meant to readers living under persecution?

_____

_____

_____

_____

_____

_____

Invitation and Response

God's Word always invites a response. Think about the way the themes of persecution, faithfulness, and perseverance speak to us today. How do they invite us to respond?

Daniel's example invites us to take stock of our own private worship habits-to honestly evaluate

how we live out our faith behind closed doors. This text also reminds us that while political leaders

and cultural pressures will come and go, God gives us the strength to endure trials and

remain faithful.

What is your evaluation of yourself based on any or all of the verses found in Daniel 6?

DANIEL 7

The latter half of Daniel will repeat the themes of previous chapters—this time on a cosmic scale. While the early chapters celebrate liberation from a lions' den, these latter chapters anticipate salvation from death itself. The early chapters deal with the kings and rulers who oppress God's people; these latter chapters address the larger forces that seek to oppress and destroy God's people.

WEEK 6, DAY 1

Listen to the story in Daniel 7 by reading it aloud several times until you become familiar with its verses, words, and phrases. Enjoy the experience of imagining the story in your mind, picturing each event as it unfolds.

WEEK 6, DAY 2

DANIEL 7

The Setting

For the modern reader, chapter 7 is where Daniel's strange visions begin. The latter half of Daniel is not nearly as familiar or inspiring as the first half, and as a result, it tends to be neglected. Yet, in many ways, chapter 7 is the central focus of the entire book. All the hero stories that have come before are expressed again in a vastly different genre—a genre which was relatively new at the time, and which was meant to bring encouragement to those living in culture's margins. While these visions seem strange to us, the image portrayed is a familiar one—the image of a God who is sovereign over this unfair and often evil world.

In the modern western world, apocalyptic imagery typically connotes a sense of doom. Yet Scripture's apocalyptic books (such as Daniel and Revelation) are meant to communicate encouragement and joy. This is a difficult concept for modern readers: why would visions of destruction bring joy? If we follow the timeline of chapter 7, we see that the Seleucids have banned religious observances in the temple and have erected an image of Zeus within it. Their armies are actively engaged against the Jewish people; violence and oppression are daily realities for those in Jerusalem. The end of the current world order would have meant an end to the oppression and injustice they experienced daily. The idea of a new kingdom replacing the current ones would have been good news and brought joy to these faithful Jews.

The Plot

The images in Daniel 7 are striking but strange to the modern reader. In this chapter, strange beasts arise from the sea and have a cosmic encounter with one who looks like a son of man. While these ideas are foreign to us, this chapter is one of the most frequently quoted passages in the New Testament. Moreover, the message of this chapter is fairly clear: God is the ultimate power in the cosmos and will defeat the forces that stand against his people. Even when things look bleak, God has not forgotten his people.

To discover the plot of Daniel 7, let's examine the passage by dividing it into seven sections. Below, summarize or paraphrase the general message or theme of each verse or grouping of verses (following the pattern provided for verses 1 and 2–7).

1. Daniel 7:1

During Belshazzar's reign, Daniel receives a vision.

_____

_____

2. Daniel 7:2–7

In his vision, Daniel sees four powerful beasts rising from the sea.

_____

_____

3. Daniel 7:8–12

_____

_____

_____

_____

_____

_____

_____

4. Daniel 7:13–14

_____

_____

_____

_____

_____

5. Daniel 7:15–18

_____
_____
_____
_____
_____
_____
_____
_____
_____

6. Daniel 7:19–25

_____
_____
_____
_____
_____
_____
_____
_____
_____

7. Daniel 7:26–28

_____
_____
_____
_____
_____
_____
_____
_____
_____

WEEK 6, DAY 3

What's Happening in the Story?

As we notice certain circumstances in the story, we will begin to see how they are similar to or different from the realities of our world. The story will become the lens through which we see the world in which we live today. In our study today, you may encounter words and/or phrases that are unfamiliar to you. Some of the particular words and translation choices for them have been explained in more detail in the **Word Study Notes**. If you are interested in even more help or detail, you can supplement this study with a Bible dictionary or other Bible study resource.

1. Daniel 7:1

This verse indicates to the reader that the book's focus has changed—though the remainder of chapter 7 is written in the first person, verse 1 remains a third-person description. This simple introduction also links these visions to Daniel, our hero from the first half of the book, but place them within the framework of a larger apocalyptic story.

2. Daniel 7:2–7

It is readily apparent that the images of the four beasts in chapter 7 are a retelling of Nebuchadnezzar's dream in chapter 2. The kingdoms that the beasts represent are the same ones revealed in the statue: the first three beasts represent the Babylonian, Median, and Persian kingdoms. The three beasts that represent these kingdoms appear together in other OT texts (Jeremiah 5:6, Hosea 13:7–8), and are used to evoke fear.[1] The description of the fourth beast is much more extensive than the descriptions of the previous three, which indicates the special importance of this beast. This fearsome beast crushes, devours, and tramples as one eating its prey. This beast also has ten horns—in Scripture, horns signify power and strength. Overall, this fourth beast is much stronger and more immediately dangerous than the preceding ones. Coins from the Seleucid Empire show rulers wearing helmets adorned with horns—this detail may have been a clue to the reader about the identity of this fourth beast.[2]

WORD STUDY NOTES #2

[1] Many have noted the use of "sea" in verse 2—in the Hebrew Bible, there is a long tradition of using the sea to symbolize chaos. For example, in the creation story, God's Spirit hovers over the face of the waters, which represents chaos. In other places, the sea is also used as a symbol for Israel's enemies. Thus, when beasts rise out of the sea, the ancient reader immediately assumes that these beasts are not friends of God's people.

[2] Scholars are divided on the identity of the fourth beast. While many want to link this beast with Rome, the majority of scholars link it with the Seleucids of second century BCE. Ultimately, such debates are not that important to how we read Daniel. Whether the fourth beast is Rome or the Seleucids, the message is still the same: whoever the oppressive power is, we must stay faithful. Even today, some readers approach Daniel in an attempt to identify the beasts or decipher predictive messages within the text. Again, such efforts fundamentally misunderstand the nature of apocalyptic literature, which is meant to bring hope to an oppressed minority—it is not predictive literature at all.

3. Daniel 7:8–12

The vivid description in this passage is meant to tell the reader something important: the white of the figure's clothing and hair signifies holiness and purity, which starkly contrasts with the actions and character of the beasts from the sea. The reference to wheels in verse 9 might be a source of confusion, since wheels are not part of our modern conception of a throne. Yet wheels were common imagery for divine thrones in the ancient world; they also recall Ezekiel's vision by the Kebar River in Ezekiel 1. The Ancient of Days then pronounces judgment on the beasts. He treats the fourth beast more severely and slays it because of the boastful words it proclaims. This recalls Belshazzar's boastful words and conduct in Daniel 5, and thus forms another connection between the earlier narratives and these visions.

92

4. Daniel 7:13–14

This is the climax of the vision, and it is among the most referenced Old Testament passages in the New Testament: After the four beasts are dispatched, Daniel sees "one like a son of man." This is among the most debated phrases in all the Bible.[1] Does it refer to a human being who ascends to the throne, or a divine figure who descends upon the clouds? Heavenly figures are associated with clouds in many eschatological texts, so the latter description seems more plausible. If this is the case, then the son of man is somehow a representative of humanity and reflects some greater human destiny. The son of man then receives authority to establish an eternal kingdom that is greater in power and justice than the discredited kingdoms that the beasts represent. It is clear that the writers of the New Testament saw Jesus as a fulfillment of this passage. While the clouds were not taken literally, Jesus's role as the representative of humanity was taken very seriously.

_____

_____

_____

_____

5. Daniel 7:15–18

These verses perfectly define the intent of the entire chapter. Daniel reacts to the vision like a reader might react—he has seen both the worst of human evil and the great throne room of God, and has been left fearful and unsettled by the experience. The angel's response is simple and comforting to Daniel as well as the reader: "The holy people of the Most High will receive the kingdom and will possess it forever." [1] This is why we can be encouraged even in the midst of the harshest trial: God is aware, God is active, and God's people will emerge victorious.

6. Daniel 7:19–25

Again, there has been considerable speculation about the identity of the fourth beast and its accompanying horns. If we retain a historical reading of the text, the fourth beast seems to refer to the Greeks and to their vestiges, the Seleucids. The ten horns, then, would represent the rulers of the empire starting with Alexander. While identifying each of the ten is difficult, the climactic horn in this passage would be Antiochus IV, the ruler who was oppressing the Jews in the second century. Some scholars reject this interpretation, arguing that nothing resembling God's kingdom was instituted after Antiochus's death. These commentators instead argue that the fourth beast is Rome, and the horns are ten kingdoms that follow Rome. In this view, the horn that issues threats is a future power that has not yet arisen. Yet this interpretation is loaded with problems as well—designating the first three beasts as historical kingdoms, then calling the fourth a manifestation of some future kingdom that no one can imagine is a bridge too far. This view also ignores the nature of apocalyptic literature—again, its purpose is not to predict and identify, but to provide comfort in difficult times. God's kingdom and reign are imminent in the midst of any trial—this is why both the second-century Jew and the modern reader can take comfort.

WORD STUDY NOTES #5

[1] The term "holy people of the Most High" can be used for either God's people on earth or angelic forces in heaven, and both are in view here. The author wants his readers to know that they are not alone and that God is acting on their behalf in ways they cannot see or appreciate.

7. Daniel 7:26–28

If the vision is meant to bring comfort, why is Daniel still troubled at the end of this chapter? Though Daniel's vision promises a divine victory, the realities of oppression remain. This chapter shows us that victory will not come easily, but only through both personal and cosmic struggle.

WEEK 6, DAY 4

The Beasts from the Sea, the Son of Man, and the Story of God

If you have a study Bible, it may have references in the margin, a middle column, or footnotes that point to other biblical texts. You may find it helpful in understanding how the whole story of God ties together to look up some of those other scriptures from time to time. Whenever we read a biblical text, it is important to ask how the text we are reading relates to the rest of the Bible.

This is not the Bible's only description of God's throne. **In the space provided below, write a short summary of how the throne in Daniel 7 relates to the other biblical passages.**

1. 1 Kings 22:19

_____

_____

_____

_____

_____

_____

_____

_____

2. Psalm 11:4

_____

_____

_____

_____

_____

_____

_____

_____

3. Psalm 45:6

_____
_____
_____
_____
_____
_____
_____
_____
_____
_____
_____
_____
_____

4. Isaiah 6:1-3

_____
_____
_____
_____
_____
_____
_____
_____
_____
_____
_____
_____
_____
_____
_____

WEEK 6, DAY 5

Daniel and Our World Today

When we enter into the intriguing narrative of Daniel 7, the story becomes the lens through which we see ourselves, our world, and God's action in our world today.

Answer these questions about how we understand ourselves, our world, and God's action in our world today.

1. In ancient Jewish literature, the sea was a symbol of chaos and evil. What is the author communicating by describing these beasts as rising from the sea?

_____

_____

_____

_____

_____

_____

_____

_____

_____

2. What sort of imagery do we have today that functions in a similar way to the sea in Daniel 7? For instance, what are some ways we can tell the good guys from the bad guys in modern literature and television?

_____

_____

_____

_____

_____

_____

_____

_____

_____

3. In which ways did Jesus fulfill the description of the son of man in Daniel 7:13–14?

_____

_____

_____

_____

_____

_____

_____

4. In the midst of intense persecution by powerful rulers, how would an ancient reader receive the promise of an eternal kingdom for God's people?

_____

_____

_____

_____

_____

_____

_____

5. If God had already promised his people an eternal kingdom, why was Daniel still troubled and unsettled at the end of this chapter?

_____

_____

_____

_____

_____

_____

_____

Invitation and Response

God's Word always invites a response. Think about the way the theme of encourage-ment in the midst of oppression speaks to us today. How does it invite us to respond?

Daniel's vision reminds us that while the evils and oppressions around us might be terrifying,

we can rest in God's promises—though the state of the world may appear bleak, our God

fights for us and will ultimately triumph.

What is your evaluation of yourself based on any or all of the verses found in Daniel 7?

DANIEL 11-12

As we approach the final chapters of Daniel and the end of our study, we would do well to recall that apocalyptic literature is not meant to predict the future. Instead, its purpose is to bring comfort to God's people by placing the events around them in context. For the ancient reader, the events described were history—a history which they lived daily.

In the end, the message of this chapter is clear: you have survived these previous kingdoms, and even if things look bleak now, you will survive the present trial as well.

WEEK 7, DAY 1

Listen to the story in Daniel 11–12 by reading it aloud several times until you become familiar with its verses, words, and phrases. Enjoy the experience of imagining the story in your mind, picturing each event as it unfolds.

WEEK 7, DAY 2

DANIEL 11-12

The Setting

These final chapters are set solidly within the second century BCE. The descriptions in chapter II read like a history of the events that transpired between the Ptolemaic Kingdom in Egypt and the Seleucid Kingdom north of Palestine. There are some who believe that II:2–39 is a futuristic prophecy that precisely foretells each of these events. But if this is true, we must also ask, why is everything past II:40 so mistaken?

We should remember that apocalyptic literature is not concerned with the future. If this is the case, then the events in II:2–39 are a description of history told from the perspective of one from the past looking forward. The setting for this chapter is the middle of a future that Daniel predicted.

The Plot

Many modern readers try to assert that Daniel is looking into the future here, and that these visions describe the end of all things. This interpretation creates more problems than it solves—a more plausible explanation is that the writer is looking at events in his lifetime and despairs of the future. Antiochus is in control, temple sacrifices have ceased, and there is an image of Zeus upon the altar—to a faithful Jew, it would seem the end is very near indeed.

The writer uses language that, at the time, would have been understood as hopeful. The people of God are not alone; there are heavenly forces who fight on their behalf, and the struggle is temporary. Ancient readers could be encouraged that if they were faithful like the heroes in Daniel, they would be rewarded.

To discover the plot of Daniel II–I2, let's examine the passage by dividing it into seven sections. **Below, summarize or paraphrase the general message or theme of each grouping of verses (following the pattern provided for 11:1–6 and 7–13).**

1. Daniel 11:1–6

In Daniel's vision, he sees four rulers arise in Persia. Another ruler rises and sees his empire broken up. A Southern kingdom attempts to form an alliance with a Northern kingdom, but is unsuccessful.

2. Daniel 11:7–13

A ruler arises from the Southern kingdom and plunders the Northern kingdom. The Northern

kingdom attempts to retaliate, but is unsuccessful. The Southern ruler is victorious in battle for

a time, but eventually, the Northern ruler reemerges with a vast army.

3. Daniel 11:14–20

4. Daniel 11:21–35

5. Daniel 11:36–45

_____
_____
_____
_____
_____
_____
_____
_____
_____

6. Daniel 12:1–4

_____
_____
_____
_____
_____
_____
_____
_____
_____

7. Daniel 12:5–13

_____
_____
_____
_____
_____
_____
_____
_____
_____

WEEK 7, DAY 3

What's Happening in the Story?

As we notice certain circumstances in the story, we will begin to see how they are similar to or different from the realities of our world. The story will become the lens through which we see the world in which we live today. In our study today, you may encounter words and/or phrases that are unfamiliar to you. Some of the particular words and translation choices for them have been explained in more detail in the **Word Study Notes**. If you are interested in even more help or detail, you can supplement this study with a Bible dictionary or other Bible study resource.

1. Daniel 11:1-6

When the writer refers to a "mighty king" in verse 3, Alexander the Great is undoubtedly in view. This is further evidenced by the reference to his kingdom being broken up and scattered to the four winds of heaven. While this is clearly symbolic language, the reference to the number four also corresponds to the four divisions of the Greek Empire that occurred after Alexander's death. These factions would fight over the remnants of Alexander's empire, and two of them would negatively impact the Jews in Palestine.

2. Daniel 11:7-13

These verses describe events that occurred between 246 BCE and approximately 200 BCE—namely, a series of campaigns and battles between the Ptolemaic Empire and the Seleucid Empire. While none of these battles were decisive, the struggle between these empires deeply impacted the Jews, since they lived between the two world powers.

3. Daniel 11:14-20

Around 198 BCE, the Seleucids pushed back the Ptolemaics and gained full control over Palestine. The Jews' holy land was then fully under Seleucid control. Having grown more ambitious, Antiochus III turned his attention to Asia Minor. However, he was soundly defeated by Rome around 190 BCE and was forced to pay tribute to Rome. He was assassinated soon after this defeat and was eventually succeeded by his son, Antiochus IV.

4. Daniel 11:21–35

This is a vital section of this chapter—everything after verse 20 refers to Antiochus IV's tragic and oppressive reign. In 168 BCE, Roman forces soundly defeated Antiochus and ended his dreams of taking over Egypt. Around the same time, there was an uprising in Jerusalem, and Antiochus took out his anger on the Jews, massacring many in the process. Seleucid forces also robbed the temple of all its valuable items. To further teach the Jews a lesson, Antiochus banned daily sacrifices and erected an altar to Zeus in the temple. The Jews were horrified by the desecration of their holy site and reacted in rage against the Seleucids, thus sparking a three-year war for independence.

_____

_____

_____

_____

_____

_____

5. Daniel 11:36–45

This section of Daniel is the most difficult to understand. Until this point, chapter 11 has aligned with historical events in Palestine. But once we come to this section, it is difficult to match the descriptions to any historical events, especially after verse 40. As we have mentioned previously, scholars take two different approaches to this section. First, some scholars read this section as a description of future events. The problem with this approach is that there is nothing in the text to indicate a transition from historical description to future prediction. Other scholars believe that these verses describe the time in which Daniel was written. In this interpretation, everything after verse 40 represents an attempt to decipher what the author's future might hold. Prophecy in the Bible is not intended to precisely describe future events, but to assure readers that God will overcome oppressive tyrants. This holds true in Daniel 11.

_____

_____

_____

_____

_____

_____

6. Daniel 12:1–4

Resurrection of the faithful is not a major part of the Old Testament, but it emerges here in a victorious declaration.[1] If God is able to complete his redemptive purposes and renew all things in the end, then all is not lost—there is hope in even the most difficult trials.[2] This declaration may be Daniel's most valuable contribution to the biblical story.

_____

_____

_____

_____

7. Daniel 12:5–13

Daniel asks how long this struggle will last, and he receives a very poetic answer. Again, our objective here is not to identify exactly which time period is being described. Instead, we glean from the man's answer that just as distress seems to gain momentum, it will be slowed, then eventually stopped. In other words, hardship and distress are temporary. Deliverance will come at the most unlikely time. And when human resources run out, God will show up. Daniel wants more information: What will be the outcome of all this? The answer is clear and firm—the linen-clothed figure tells Daniel to go on with his life. This is still the answer today—in times of hardship we must go on with life, remembering that the hardship will be temporary and our obedience will be rewarded. The man makes a cryptic reference to 1,290 days, and then to 1,335 days.[1] It is difficult to match these exact timespans with any events that we know of. However, both of these numbers are very close to three and a half years—or the time, times, and half a time from 7:25. This length of time roughly corresponds to the duration of the Jews' struggle after the desecration of the temple.

_____

_____

_____

_____

WORD STUDY NOTES #6

[1] There are other, subtler references to resurrection in the Old Testament, though none are as clear as Daniel 12. Some texts allude to vindication after death (Job 19:25–27); others describe life after death in vague terms (Psalm 73:23–26). The other most blatant reference is probably Isaiah 26:19, which states, "your dead will live . . . their bodies will rise." Daniel 12 offers promises of deliverance, judgment, and everlasting life, which are themes Revelation will expand upon in the New Testament.

[2] This principle aligns with the ancient Jews' view of the cosmos. In their perspective, there are struggles in the heavenly realms that correspond to earthly struggles; Michael leads the heavenly forces against the forces that oppose against God's people and are led by Belial. We should not mistake this for a literal description of events—it is simply a way to express the struggles of God's people and illustrate how God actively defends them. We find similar descriptions in Ephesians, which takes these themes and expands upon them.

WORD STUDY NOTES #7

[1] The "abomination that causes desolation" is usually identified in one of two ways. Some assert that this phrase refers to some future event that will significantly impact God's people. This does not seem likely given how well these latter chapters match actual historical events. Instead, this phrase probably describes the setting up of Zeus's image in the temple. The exact identification of dates and events is less important than this final section's overall message: Believers may have to suffer now, but that suffering is only temporary—God will make all things right.

WEEK 7, DAY 4

The Final Visions and the Story of God

If you have a study Bible, it may have references in the margin, a middle column, or footnotes that point to other biblical texts. You may find it helpful in understanding how the whole story of God ties together to look up some of those other scriptures from time to time. Whenever we read a biblical text, it is important to ask how the text we are reading relates to the rest of the Bible.

This is not the only place in which the Bible describes God's victory over evil forces in grand, cosmic terms. **In the space provided below, write a short summary of how this theme from Daniel 11–12 is demonstrated in the other biblical passages.**

1. **Romans 8:1–27**

_____

_____

_____

_____

_____

_____

_____

_____

2. **Ephesians 3:1–13**

_____

_____

_____

_____

_____

_____

_____

_____

3. Colossians 2:6–15

_____

_____

_____

_____

_____

_____

_____

_____

4. Revelation 5

_____

_____

_____

_____

_____

_____

_____

_____

5. Revelation 20:1–10

_____

_____

_____

_____

_____

_____

_____

_____

WEEK 7, DAY 5

Daniel and Our World Today

When we enter into the intriguing narrative of Daniel 11–12, the story becomes the lens through which we see ourselves, our world, and God's action in our world today.

Answer these questions about how we understand ourselves, our world, and God's action in our world today.

1. This section of Daniel contains a promise of resurrection. How would this promise have encouraged readers who were struggling with intense persecution?

_____

_____

_____

_____

_____

_____

_____

_____

_____

2. In the final chapter, Daniel is told to "go [his] way." What is valuable about the advice to keep on living in the midst of persecution?

_____

_____

_____

_____

_____

_____

_____

_____

_____

3. The linen-clothed figure in chapter 12 states that some will be purified in the difficult times, but "the wicked will continue to be wicked." What do you think of this observation?

_____

_____

_____

_____

_____

_____

_____

_____

4. Why do so many people want to find predictions about the future in the Bible? What are the dangers of this approach?

_____

_____

_____

_____

_____

_____

_____

_____

5. Which is more important: exact details about the future, or the message that God will defeat evil and reward his people for their faithfulness? Why?

_____

_____

_____

_____

_____

_____

_____

_____

Invitation and Response

God's Word always invites a response. Think about the way the theme of living in the midst of trials speaks to us today. How does it invite us to respond?

This text reminds us that though we are surrounded by suffering, war, and political turmoil,

the Lord is our defender. It invites us to rest in his promises and to live our lives for him,

regardless of what temporary trials may afflict us.

What is your evaluation of yourself based on any or all of the verses found in Daniel 11–12?